Seasons of

Also by the same author and available from the Canterbury Press

Watching for the Kingfisher: Poems and prayers
'This . . . can be returned to again and again, each time discovering a new gem.'
The Good Bookstall

Love is the Meaning: Growing in faith with Julian of Norwich

Forthcoming
Come, Emmanuel: Exploring Advent and Christmas

www.canterburypress.co.uk

Seasons of Grace

Inspirational resources for the Christian year

Ann Lewin

Published in 2011 by the Canterbury Press Norwich
Editorial office
13–17 Long Lane,
London, EC1A 9PN, UK

Canterbury Press is an imprint of Hymns Ancient and Modern
Ltd (a registered charity)
13A Hellesdon Park Road, Norwich,
Norfolk, NR6 5DR, UK

www.scm-canterburypress.co.uk

Previously published under the title *Words by the Way*, by Inspire,
an imprint of the Methodist Publishing House

British Library Cataloguing in Publication data

A catalogue record for this book is available
from the British Library

978 1 84825 090 1

Printed and bound in Great Britain by
CPI Antony Rowe, Chippenham, Wiltshire

Contents

Section 2 Lent to Pentecost

Section 3 Ordinary Time

Dedication

This book is dedicated to Ron, Nigel and Gary, whose friendship and prayerful support over the years have been a great source of encouragement.

There are also many other individuals and groups who, by inviting me to lead events or address a variety of audiences, have given me opportunities to explore fresh ways of communicating the gospel. I have received many blessings from these companions on the way, and I am immensely grateful to them for their challenge and their insights.

Thanksgiving

Given so much,
What have I done to
Deserve it?
Nothing,
Absolutely nothing.
No wonder my heart
Dances.

Ann Lewin, in *Watching for the Kingfisher*, p. 130

Acknowledgements

I am grateful to many people who have contributed to the production of this book.

Gary Philbrick read the text in preparation, and made many helpful suggestions from a potential user's point of view. In addition, he has come to my rescue on several occasions when my computer has tried to get the upper hand.

I am grateful to Canterbury Press for undertaking to publish this new, enlarged, edition of *Words by the Way,* and I remain grateful to the staff at the *Inspire* imprint of the Methodist Publishing House, now discontinued, for publishing the first edition.

Foreword

It is important for Christians to make connections between our experience of church worship and our ongoing prayer and spiritual life. *Seasons of Grace* gives us a good opportunity to do this. Taking us through the cycle of the Church's year, Ann Lewin offers us both a resource for personal reflection (with encouragement about how we might approach our everyday praying) and an imaginative range of liturgical material that picks up the themes and imagery of each season in turn.

The shape of the Church's year reminds us of the great drama of our creation and salvation, and every time and season contains an invitation to place our own story, and that of our world, within the unfolding story found in Scripture. Yet we can sometimes be so busy or preoccupied that the richness and flavour of the different parts of the Christian year simply pass us by, and we miss the spiritual treasures within the fabric of each particular season. Ann's book may help us to recover some of these things, such as the wonderful sense of anticipation in Advent, the beauty and mystery of Epiphany, the prayerful possibilities of Good Friday, and the significance of lesser known festivals such as Lammastide.

In her introduction Ann says that she hopes her material 'will spark off creativity in people looking for fresh ways to present truths about God and ourselves'. I can envisage several ways in which this could happen. Some readers who feel that their prayer life is in a rut may find that this book opens up new ways of relating to God through the year. The practical suggestions on pages 18–19 would be a good place to start for those who are not sure where to go next in their prayer life. In addition, I am sure that people responsible for leading worship, or events such as Quiet Days, will welcome the liturgical material and suggestions. This book might also inspire a group within a congregation to organize a special event for carers (pp. 199ff), the setting up of a Quiet Garden (pp. 202ff), or a day exploring the teaching of someone like Julian of Norwich (pp. 192ff). Ann's ideas may also encourage readers to take other creative initiatives of their own, using the sort of outlines and practical suggestions that she gives.

This book is earthed in the realities of daily life, and its journey through the seasons frequently connects us with ordinary experiences. At the same time, there are many glimpses of heaven, for example in the section for Easter Eve:

Lord Christ, set us on fire,
burn from us all that dims your light;
kindle an answering flame in lives around,
that darkness may be driven back,
and glory stream into this world,
transforming it with light. (p. 134)

Ann has the knack of offering us lots of ideas without trying to control or dictate what we do. That is probably because of her own deep understanding of what prayer is about:

Prayer is like watching for the
Kingfisher. All you can do is
Be where he is likely to appear and
Wait. (p. 27)

Prayer and worship are about waiting on God with open and generous hearts, rather than trying to control God or make things happen to suit ourselves. One way in which we can grow in this openness to God is when our corporate worship and our personal prayer flow into each other and nourish each other. By using this book we may find that dream becoming more of a reality.

Angela Ashwin
Writer and lecturer on spirituality

Introduction

This book is a collection of material I have devised and used over several years. It contains reflections on the significance of seasons and festivals, as well as schemes for use in Workshops, Quiet Days, Retreats and Courses. There are suggestions for liturgy also, including some Eucharistic Prayers, and a simple order for the Eucharist in which these prayers can be used. The prayers were originally written for specific groups, but they have been adapted for other use also. My aim is always to use as few words as possible to say what needs to be said, and to leave space for people to respond to God as God moves them.

The first two sections of the book reflect the events of Jesus' life as the Church's year unfolds. The third section is more diverse, offering responses to the opportunities daily life affords to meet God.

Much of what I offer draws from my own writing in *Watching for the Kingfisher*, published in an enlarged edition by Canterbury Press in 2009. This edition combines some new work with poems previously published in *Candles and Kingfishers* and *Flashes of Brightness* published by the Methodist Publishing House.

I hope that what I offer here will spark off creativity in people looking for fresh ways to present truths about God and ourselves as we explore the riches of God's love anew, year by year.

Ann Lewin
May 2011

Section 1

Advent to Candlemas

Advent

There's little doubt about what most of us will be doing in the next four weeks – the Christmas rush to get everything organized, cards written, gifts bought and sent, the preparation of food, plans about whose turn it is to go visiting, and anxieties about who'll be offended if we don't pay them enough attention . . . The rush is on, and it's not surprising that there's often a hint of panic in people's conversations – 'I'll never be ready!'

In four weeks it'll all be over, in five a new year will have brought us another set of resolutions, in six the decorations will have come down, the furniture of life will be back in place, and we'll be back to – what? Will life be just the same, or will we be changed? If we take Advent seriously, I hope we *will* be changed, because we shall have had the opportunity to reflect again on what it means to say that God came into the world in the humility of the birth at Bethlehem, and that he still comes into the world in all its mess and pain and joy, longing for us to recognize him.

Advent is a godsend, a gift which stops us in our tracks, and makes us realize that we hold dual citizenship (of this world and the kingdom) in awkward tension. We are part of the scene – Christians sometimes appear to be rather superior about what we call commercialization, and say that the real Christmas isn't about that. But the real Christmas is about precisely that: it's about God coming into the real world, not to a sanitized stable as we portray it in carols and on Christmas cards, but to a world that needed, and still needs, mucking out. Advent reminds us that the kingdom has other themes to add to the celebration, themes that are there in the Scripture readings for the season: Repent, be ready, keep awake, he comes.

Advent reminds us that not only do we live in two worlds, the one that appears to be going mad all around us, and the one that lives by the kingdom of God's values, but that we operate in two different time scales, in chronological time, and beyond it. And the point of intersection is *now*. Passages of Scripture read during Advent, and the *Prayer Book* collect for Advent which is often used, remind us that *now* is the time when we have to cast away the works of darkness, and put on the armour of light. *Now* is when we meet God, because we have no other time.

At whatever level we operate, it's a time for preparation. And whatever else we have to do, there are only so many *praying* days to Christmas. It is prayer that gives us the opportunity to focus our recognition of God in every part of our lives. Prayer is not just what we do in what we call our prayer time. Prayer is how we give our relationship with God a chance to grow and develop and, just like any other relationship, it needs time. We don't stop being related when we are not with the person concerned. We don't stop being a wife, husband, child, parent or friend when that person is out of sight, or when we are concentrating on something else. But we become less of a related person if we never give them time.

So, Advent says, make time, create a space so that our understanding of God's love for us, and our love for God in response can grow. The world is saying, 'Get on with it – don't wait for Christmas to hold the celebrations.' Advent says, 'Wait, be still, alert and expectant.'

Some people find it helpful to have a focal point for their stillness; perhaps a lit candle. Any candle will do, but there are candles with the days marked on them, so that we don't have any excuse for not remembering. And using a candle like this reminds us that before there were clocks people used candles to measure time. Christmas is bound up with time as well as eternity. We're celebrating God becoming involved in our world in Jesus, and God invites us to make time for him.

The shopping days will come to an end – there will come a moment when we really can't do any more. But the point of the praying days is that we get into the habit of remembering God who comes to us every day, and longs for us to respond with our love and service.

Eucharistic Prayer for Advent

Lord God, you come to us
in the simplicity of a baby,
yet are greater by far than our imagining:
Come to us, Lord.

Lord Christ, you hide your ways from
the proud,
yet reveal your truth to those of a
childlike spirit:
Come to us, Lord.

Lord Spirit, you overthrow the powerful,
yet empower the humble and open of heart:
Come to us, Lord.

Come to us now in your vulnerable strength,
as we remember Jesus,
who brought wholeness and life
through his death and resurrection.
On the night before he died,
he took bread and wine, blessed them
and gave them to his friends, saying,
'This is my body, this is my blood.
Eat and drink to remember me.'

Come freshly to us, living God;
bring in your kingdom of justice and love:
Your kingdom come.

Heal us, that we may be whole in your service:
Your kingdom come.

Teach us, that we may be surprised into truth:
Your kingdom come.

For you are the God who longs to set us free
to love and serve you wholeheartedly:
Your kingdom come in us, Lord,
and transform the world
to your praise and glory. Amen.

Have you got room?

'Posada' is the Spanish word for 'Inn', and it gives its name to an activity which has become quite popular during Advent, as a way of engaging people in preparing for Christmas. It originated in a Mexican custom when children dressed as Mary and Joseph would go from house to house during Advent, asking people if they had any room, prompting them to think about the Christmas story. The Church Army adapted the idea in the UK, initially as a way of raising funds, and suggested that instead of children, crib figures should be sent round from house to house, spending a night wherever people were willing to give them hospitality. Their presence could be an opportunity for gathering friends and neighbours together to spend some time reflecting on their preparations for celebrating the birth of Christ. The idea has caught on, and been developed in many different ways, involving schools and local shops as well as church members. Sometimes only Mary and Joseph make the journey with a donkey, sometimes all the crib figures go their separate ways, joining together on Christmas Eve to form the crib in a church or other meeting place. Many people find it convenient to use knitted figures, and if lots of people are involved, several sets of figures can be employed. People might also be encouraged to make their own figures as part of the process.

Here are some prayers which could be used as the figures arrive at each resting place:

Welcoming the figures
Heavenly Father,
as we welcome Mary and Joseph
to be with us for a while,
we pray that we will know your presence with us
in all our preparations to celebrate
the birth of your Son,

and that the sense of your presence
will grow in us in all the days to come, **Amen.**

For travellers
God of the journey,
as we remember Joseph and Mary
on their way to Bethlehem,
we pray for all who travel
by road and rail,
in the air or on the sea.
Protect them from danger,
and bring them safely
to their journey's end. **Amen.**

For all expecting a child
Father, Mother God,
we ask your blessing on all
who are preparing to be parents.
May the birth be accomplished safely,
and new life nurtured with wisdom and love,
for his sake who became a child for us. **Amen.**

For children
Heavenly Father,
we thank you for children,
for their joy, their trust and their simplicity.
Be with them, we pray, as they grow.
May they always know that they are loved
by you, and by those to whom
you have entrusted their care. **Amen.**

For homeless people
Loving God,
we pray for all who are
homeless as your Son was:
for refugees and asylum seekers;
for all who have been driven

from their homes and their lands
by cruel leaders;
for all in our own country who sleep rough,
and all for whom no one cares.
Touch them with your love, dear Lord,
and help us to do what we can
to show your love to them,
not just at Christmas
but throughout the year. **Amen.**

For people who find Christmas difficult
Generous God,
we pray for all who will find it hard to
celebrate Christmas this year.
May our eyes be open to recognize the lonely
and all who feel excluded from the celebrations
because they have few resources.
Help us to be generous in assisting where we can. **Amen.**

For animals
Creator God,
we thank you for all the animals
which share this planet with us.
We thank you for our pets,
and all the creatures whose company we enjoy.
Especially today we thank you for the animals
which help us and serve us in many different ways.
May we always treat them with kindness and respect. **Amen.**

For ourselves
Lord Jesus,
open our minds and our hearts, that we may
welcome you afresh into our lives this Christmas,
and keep close to you in the coming year. **Amen.**

Eucharistic Prayer – the kingdom

Lord God,
your kingdom is here and not yet,
hidden, yet ours for the seeking:
Your kingdom come.

Your kingdom requires of us total commitment,
and gives us unlimited freedom:
Your kingdom come.

Your kingdom turns our values upside down,
for your King rules through suffering love:
Your kingdom come.

With angels and archangels,
and all whose lives
have been changed by your kingdom,
we praise you, saying:
Holy, holy, holy Lord,
king of joy and love,
heaven and earth are full of your glory,
all praise to your name.

Come to us now, most loving God,
as we remember Jesus, who
on the night before he died,
took bread and wine, blessed them,
and gave them to his friends, saying,
'This is my body, this is my blood.
Eat and drink, all of you.'

Come freshly to us now, Lord God.
Open our eyes to the signs of your kingdom:
Your kingdom come.

Call us again to commit ourselves to your service:
Your kingdom come.

Send your Holy Spirit,
that your life and vitality may flow through us,
and change the lives of all we meet:
Your kingdom come in us, Lord,
and transform the world,
to your praise and glory. Amen.

Thinking about prayer

'Have you done your practice? Have you said your prayers?'

Those are two questions I remember from my childhood. Odd questions . . . no one in the house could have failed to notice whether I had done my practice. And my mother was always in the house. The other question seemed a bit intrusive. Whether I'd said my prayers or not seemed to be my affair, not anyone else's. But my discomfort at being asked the question arose more from the fact that on the occasion I remember, I had to say 'no'. And I got the distinct impression that that was the wrong answer!

Reflecting later, I realized that these were not really questions at all, but a bit of parental control, making sure that I did the important things – rather like 'Have you cleaned your teeth?' And further reflection, much later on, made me think that as questions, they entirely missed the point. Doing my practice, saying my prayers were not activities for their own sake, to be done, ticked off for the day and then forgotten about until the next parental nudge; they both led on to something greater. Piano practice was important because it was part of becoming more musical – something those within earshot must have hoped would happen sooner, rather than later. And saying my prayers was part of growing more prayerful, part of establishing that relationship with God which is the foundation of all Christian living. I wonder if it would have been more helpful if I had been asked 'Have you become more musical today? Have you become more prayerful?'

Prayer is an expression of our relationship with God – and one of the other things about it that I eventually realized is that *saying* my prayers, like practising scales, was only the beginning: my practice needed to spill over into the whole of my life. Because that is what relationships are like. We don't stop being related when we are not consciously present with the person with whom we are in relationship. The relationship continues as we go about the ordinary things of life. We may think of the person we relate to from time to time – 'John would be interested in this; I must remember to tell Mary . . .' And from time to time, regularly, we need time with the other person to catch up, get to know them better, enjoy their company. I know that I don't play the piano nearly as well now that I don't practise. We all know of relationships that drift or founder because we don't make time for them.

So our prayer time is the time when we practise the presence of God, so that *all* our life may be filled with the presence of God. Most people think that behaviour matters and prayer helps it. The truth is that prayer matters, and behaviour tests it.[1]

One of the odd things about our Christian life is that on the whole we don't talk about prayer. I had piano lessons which didn't just test how I was getting on, but gave me and the teacher a chance to look at techniques that would help – a difficult passage would become easier to cope with if I sorted the fingering out, or a piece of music might come to life if I played some of it more quietly, and didn't just hit the notes . . . But I didn't have much help with learning to pray. It was something that on the whole I was left to get on with. We went to church, there was the odd sermon, but I don't remember anyone saying to me, 'How are you getting on with your prayer life?' So I suppose I grew up thinking that I was supposed to know about prayer, and that everyone else already knew. That is what we do think, probably. We look around and see everyone else devoutly concentrating, and don't realize that behind the closed eyes and clasped hands, there is as much confusion and inattention as there is in us.

There is a skit by Joyce Grenfell in which she is shown in church singing a hymn: 'Calm and untroubled are my thoughts' – and then we realize that she is singing what she is actually thinking about – she forgot to turn the gas down under the saucepan of chicken bones she was turning into stock; she imagines the pan boiling dry, the stove, then the house, catching fire; where will they sleep tonight? If she goes home now, she might be in time to save the picture which is supposed to be a Picasso, though she'd much rather save her photograph album . . . She turns to her husband and sings, 'I suppose you didn't think to check the gas? No, I didn't think you would have.' The skit ends with her singing again, 'Calm and untroubled are my thoughts'.

It's funny not just because it's Joyce Grenfell, but because it rings true for us all. We all find it difficult to concentrate, to find time – we get stuck in ways of praying that perhaps we need to grow on from. We have to learn to move from having a time of prayer to having a life of prayer. That takes practice. Unlike the piano practice, there are no exams – we're not going to be better than the people who've only passed Grade III. The aim is not to be 'good' at prayer – I don't know what that would mean – but to be faithful in establishing the prayerfulness of the whole of life. There is nothing that can't be prayerful. If we can think of anything that can't be prayerful, perhaps we need to question whether we should be doing it at all.

Nothing that can't be prayerful. There's the story of two monks who argued about whether you could drink coffee and pray at the same time. They couldn't agree, so they went off to ask their spiritual directors for advice. When they came back, they still couldn't agree. One monk said, 'My director said, "No, on no account must you let anything interfere with prayer."' The other monk said, 'That's odd, my director didn't think there was a problem at all. What did you ask?'

The first monk said, 'I asked if I could drink coffee while I was praying, and my director got quite cross with me.'

The other laughed. 'Oh, I asked whether I could pray while I was drinking coffee.'

It's all about changing our attitudes, about growing into a deeper understanding. What we are about is coming closer to the God who loves us – and our response to that love can be expressed in the words of Julian of Norwich, that wise woman from the fourteenth century. She prayed, 'God, of your goodness give us yourself; for if we ask anything that is less, we shall always be in want. Only in you we have all.'[2]

Notes

1. After William Temple, 'The proper relation in thought between prayer and conduct is not that conduct is supremely important and prayer may help it, but that prayer is supremely important, and conduct tests it.' From *Christus Veritas*, published Macmillan, London 1924. Quoted by Gordon Mursell in *English Spirituality: From 1700 to the Present Day*, vol. 2, p. 373, SPCK.
2. *Revelation of Divine Love*, Long Text ch. 5.

Material for a workshop on ways of praying

The material on pp. 18–19 has been used in many different ways: as the basis for a day, an evening, a Lent course, and for a retreat. The intention is to broaden people's understanding of prayer, to give them space to explore different ways of praying, and to have the opportunity to talk about their own prayer life, its joys and difficulties, in a way that we don't often have the chance to do.

No one comes to this subject as an expert, but we all have experience, and it is helpful to share it – if only because it is such a relief to find that other people's experience is often uncannily like our own.

It is helpful to begin by asking people to talk to their neighbour for a few minutes, identifying what they hope to get out of the event. After that, it is easier to have a general discussion in the group, and list any points people want to raise.

Often, an inability to concentrate is high on the list. It is worth dealing with that problem early in the proceedings. We don't concentrate on anything for very long – mostly we have a lot of things on our minds, and we juggle with them to prioritize. We don't suddenly change when we decide to spend time in prayer! But we also know that sometimes we get caught up in something, and don't know where the time has gone. Setting aside time for prayer means that we put ourselves where God can catch our attention, and then we can leave the prayer to God. For prayer is always a gift, it is God who prays in us and transforms us, rather than we who achieve great heights of devotion. We don't have to beat ourselves up about the fact that we are creatures with a short attention span – when we find our thoughts wandering off, we can gently bring ourselves back to God. And the more we practise doing that, the more natural it becomes to find ourselves aware of God's presence.

How much time we can give to consideration of the various ways of praying depends on the nature of the event, but it is always important to give people time to explore for themselves, and have a time for comments and questions. We don't have to do everything on one occasion – an introduction to what is possible may lead fruitfully to follow-up sessions.

The ways of praying illustrated are arranged on the sheet so that those around the edges are methods which require some time to be set aside. Between them are the ideas we can put into practice as we go about daily life. The candle stands for Christ at the centre, and reminds us that prayer is the expression of our relationship with God as we have been shown him in Jesus, and in God we have all. Much has already been written about the ways of praying illustrated, but ideas about exploring some of them further follow the illustration.

Find a way that works for you

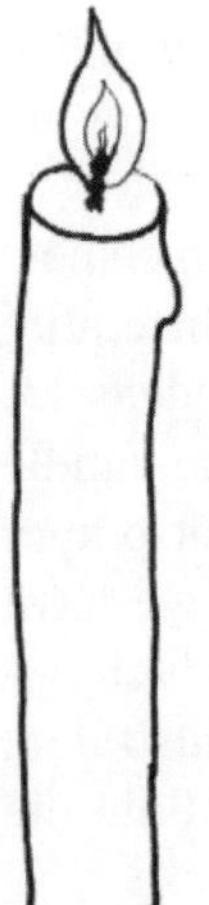

Light a candle

Reflect that Jesus is the light of the world.

Remember your baptism – you have been called from the darkness to live in the light.

Celebrate!

Light a prayer for someone – others will draw strength from your light.

Write a Psalm

Look at a Psalm (Psalm 77 perhaps). Notice its absolute honesty about feelings, and what it says about God. Try writing your own.

Spend time with an icon

Let it speak to you, draw you into its inner meaning.

Go for a walk

Look at what is around you. Give thanks for what is good. Look at the Benedicite (in Anglican Morning Prayer service) Make up your own version:
O . . .
bless ye the Lord . . .
Touch – enjoy the texture of tree-trunk, stone, fabric . . .
Listen – enjoy the peace, or use the sounds you hear as material for prayer: police siren or birdsong can each start you off.

Read the paper

Don't get sucked in – set statements of faith against reported news, (the Psalms will give you ideas). Put your arm around those who make the news, and hold them before God.

Sing and make melody to the Lord. Laments and protests too.

Adoration
Confession
Thanksgiving
Supplication

These **ACTS** are a good basis for prayer

Draw or paint

Go on a pilgrimage

Pilgrimage is about visiting places and recognizing that God has been at work there. You can go to holy places: you can also recognize the holiness of ordinary places. Try looking at the street you live in, the rooms of your home, different parts of your body. Remember God is concerned about each of them – make the connections.

Carry a prayer around

Use it when your mind is in neutral – at the supermarket checkout, in a traffic jam – much more constructive than cursing delay! The Jesus prayer* or Taizé chants are good.

**Lord Jesus Christ, Son of God, have mercy.*

Spend time

thinking about what you have read in the Bible or another book which points you to God.

Use an 'office' –

morning or evening prayer. Make up a basic kit for yourself – Psalm, reading, prayers.

Practise stillness

Let God have a chance. Don't try to think – gently repeat a short prayer, let it focus your mind, take you deep.

Dance! If your joints will let you.

Let go and let God

Using the Psalms

The Psalms are a very rich resource, tested and tried in many situations. People often have their favourite quotations, which they call to mind as appropriate. As well as providing words of comfort or encouragement, the Psalms show us a way of bringing all our feelings to God. They give us words to use to express our joy and trust; they also give us words to use when we are angry or in despair. They offer us a model of setting alongside the awfulness of life a statement about God, sometimes linked with a '*nevertheless*'. They do not ask us to resolve our problems by saying that everything is going to be all right. They ask us to face the difficulty, and hold it in tension with what we believe about God, and wait.

We are sometimes worried by the intensity of our feelings, and think that we can't let God know how angry and violent we feel. After all, 'nice' people don't think or say the things we would really like to express! But actually there is nothing in the Christian gospel about being 'nice'. There is plenty about being loving and just, and straight in our dealings with others. Sometimes the only right response is anger. There is nothing about us that God does not already know, and nothing about us that will stop God loving us, whatever we feel.

It is important to look at the whole of a Psalm, and not leave out the hard verses. Liturgically we may need to omit some verses: it would probably not be very edifying for someone who had just dropped in to see what our worship was like, to hear everyone saying, 'Break their teeth, O God!' (Psalm 58.4). For personal use, though, we need to see the Psalms as they are, and experience the liberation of learning that honesty with God can be the beginning of a vigorous relationship with him.

It is a useful exercise sometimes to write a psalm for ourselves. There is great value in writing out what we feel, especially in times of anger or bewilderment or despair. The process can help us to see the situation in a more objective way, and often cuts it down to size, preventing our imaginations from running away with us in unhelpful ways.

This is how one person at a workshop responded to the invitation to write a psalm.

He was grieving the death of his daughter from leukaemia, and reflected on Psalm 137, set in the Book of Common Prayer for use on the 28th evening of the month.

His reflection centred on the last verse of the Psalm: 'Blessed shall he be that taketh thy children: and throweth them against the stones.'

28th Evening

You took our child, God. You threw her on the rocks of cancer. You tortured her little body with surgery and chemotherapy and radiotherapy, and you tortured us with hope. You did that for eighteen months. And then for a year you mocked us, as her hair grew back and that sharp and musical mind flourished as never before.

And then you struck, and the laughter died in our throats. At least you spared us hope the second time.

Now we could only watch with her, and wait, as the talents which seemed about to burst so joyfully from Hannah withered and died. And we talked together of what would be, knowing that as we did, it was only of what might have been.

You threw her against the stones one last time, and she died on the 28th evening – just ten days before her sixth birthday. And I cannot forgive you for that, God. Hannah has, that I know. For all that she endured at your hands, she still went on loving you. Your abused child. Because she didn't know any better. Thank God I do not have her faith, her incapacity to hate.

What were you doing? I was the one with her. I was the one who held her in my arms for the injections. I was the one who calmed her fears during the nose bleeds.

Who held You?
Who gave you strength?
Who so encompassed you around with love that it flowed out from you to Hannah without despair? She could only love me so trustingly because she knew what a Father's love could be.

By the waters of Babylon I sat down and wept – with you.
With you from the first morning to the 28th Evening.
And with you now
And with Hannah now
And she with me though I no longer weep for her.
Though still I shall weep with you whenever you visit the waters of Babylon.

Robin Harger
(used with permission)

Praying with icons

Icons are not just pictures, they are windows into the world beyond. They play an important part in the prayer and worship of Eastern Orthodox Christians. They are stylized, painted according to ancient custom by rules handed down through the generations, and are always the fruit of prayerful attention to God. At first sight they may not be very attractive to western eyes, but paying attention to them may draw us deeper into the mystery they represent.

They are painted (Orthodox Christians would say 'written') using a different scheme of perspective from that to which westerners have become accustomed. In western post-Renaissance painting, the lines of perspective lead the eye to a distant point. In many icons, the perspective is reversed, so that our attention becomes focused in front of the icon, between us and it. Sometimes it seems as though the icon is looking at us, instead of the other way round. There is a sense that we are being engaged by the subject. The icons of Mary with the infant Christ, for example, invite us to contemplate the child – the angle of Mary's head, the position of her hands, and the way she holds the child, all point to him: we are invited to give Christ the central place in our worship. The icon of the Holy Trinity gives the impression that the three persons of the Trinity are all paying attention to each other – look at the angle of their heads – and the gap in the front of the circle invites us to join in the conversation.

There is a sense of stillness in icons. The eyes of the characters portrayed seem to be contemplating some inner truth. Mouths are often small, and eyes large – the key to spiritual growth is watchfulness and attention, rather than talking a lot.

It takes time to appreciate what God may be saying to us through an icon – what we have to do is be still before it, and wait.

There are several books which can help us to understand icons better, among them:

John Baggley, *Doors of Perception*, Mowbray, 1987.

John Baggley, *Festival Icons for the Christian Year*, Mowbray, 1987.

Jim Forrest, *Praying with Icons*, Orbis, 1997.

Henri Nouwen, *Behold the Beauty of the Lord – Praying with Icons*, Ave Maria Press, 1987.

Using silence

> 'In quietness and in trust shall be your strength.' (Isaiah 30.15)
>
> 'For God alone my soul waits in silence.' (Psalm 62.1)
>
> 'Come away to a deserted place all by yourselves and rest a while.' (Mark 6.31)

There is much in Scripture about God coming to people in stillness. Our difficulty is that modern life tries to keep us constantly on the go, and we are in the habit of filling our airwaves with noise. We have to make a conscious effort to get away from life's muzak and listen. When we do that, we discover another problem: we don't always want to engage in stillness because we fear what we may discover about ourselves. We have to remember that God knows us in the depths of our being, and loves us as we are: 'You are precious in my sight, and honoured, and I love you' (Isaiah 43.4). That doesn't mean that we don't need to change, but that we don't need to wait until we have before we can enjoy God's company. If there are areas within ourselves which need to be dealt with, it may be wise to wait until we can work with a trusted guide.

Stillness and silence are states we have to learn to relax into, rather than screwing ourselves up to find them, and there are various techniques which may help:

- Find a place where you can be relaxed, yet alert. Some people find it helpful to have a particular place in house or garden which they regard as their prayer place.
- Decide how long you are going to spend in this way of prayer.
- Light a candle, play some music, use a relaxation exercise to help mind and body to settle.

- Read a short passage of Scripture, select a thought or phrase from it; or use a sentence from a hymn or a prayer. Repeat the phrase gently, in time with your breathing.
- Let yourself become still; let God hold you in love.
- When thoughts do wander, gently re-establish the phrase (or 'rhythm prayer' as some people call it) and allow yourself to become still again. Don't worry if your thoughts wander off. We are usually not very good at concentrating in the normal course of events, and we don't suddenly change when we decide to pray. Wandering thoughts are not something to feel guilty about.
- At the end of the allotted time, gently bring yourself back to awareness of what is around you. (You may need to set a timer or an alarm, but put it in another room, so that it doesn't jolt you back into ordinariness.) Perhaps play some music again, to help you adjust.
- Say a brief prayer of thanksgiving for the opportunity to be still, and for God's presence with you.

Don't worry if nothing much seems to have happened. Prayer is God's gift to us: what we have to do is open ourselves up to the possibility of receiving the gift, and leave the rest to God.

Disclosure

Prayer is like watching for the
Kingfisher. All you can do is
Be where he is likely to appear and
Wait.
Often, nothing much happens;
There is space, silence and
Expectancy.
No visible sign, only the
Knowledge that he's been there
And may come again.
Seeing or not seeing cease to matter,
You have been prepared,
But sometimes, when you've almost
Stopped expecting it
A flash of brightness
Gives encouragement.[1]

Note

1. *Watching for the Kingfisher*, p. 31.

Carrying prayer around

When people talk about prayer, it often sounds like a specialized activity. There are many techniques and methods we can use. But as we grow in prayerfulness, we have to learn to take prayer out of the speciality range into general use, to learn how prayer can be a way of life.

Paul said, 'Pray without ceasing' (1 Thessalonians 5.17). We might feel like responding with, 'You must be joking – I've got far too much to do to be able to indulge in prayer all the time.' And at one level that's true. There are things we have to do which demand all our attention. I'm glad when people do pay attention to what they are doing. I wouldn't thank my dentist, for example, if he did anything other than keep his mind on the job!

There is an old saying in Latin, *laborare est orare* – to work is to pray. Doing what we have to do wholeheartedly is prayer. When our lives are offered to God, every part of our life is part of that offering.

Brother Lawrence was a Carmelite monk in the seventeenth century. He was well known for his holiness and his awareness of the presence of God. He wasn't a scholar or a choir monk, he worked in the kitchen amidst all the demands of a busy monastery. People often think of monasteries as places of calm – those who live in them know that it isn't quite like that. Communities, like families, have their tensions. In his time monasteries were very busy places, a cross between a Travelodge and McDonalds, catering not just for those who lived there, but for visitors and pilgrims too.

Brother Lawrence believed that it was important to relate all his life to God, work and prayer alike. He said that his method was simple: he would go to the times of prayer required by his monastery, then he would do his work, asking God to help him to stay in God's presence, and do his work well. When he finished his work, he would examine himself as to how well he had done it. If well, he thanked God, if not, he asked pardon and, without being discouraged, continued to try to stay aware of God's presence. 'The time of business does not differ with me from the time of prayer, and in the noise and clutter of my kitchen, while several persons are at the same time calling for different things, I possess God in as great tranquillity as if I were on my knees at the Blessed Sacrament.'

That is the challenge for us all, to learn to live our lives aware of God's presence. Easier said than done! Brother Lawrence's way of prayer is sometimes called 'The practice of the presence of God'. If we are wondering how on earth we can do it, it is worth remembering that the word that we hear as a noun 'practice', is also a verb, 'practise'.

We have to establish the habit of remembering that there is a connection between God and ourselves wherever we are: walking around, relaxing with friends, shopping – *now* is the time we meet God. Two simple prayers are enough to carry around with us: 'Thank God', and 'Lord, have mercy'. These are the responses we can make to all the circumstances of our lives, for God is concerned with the painful experiences and the hard questions just as much as with the joys and delights.

And God is concerned with the chores too. We can, for example, transform our wait in the supermarket queue by using our imaginations about the people and the trolleys around us. The old man with a loaf and a tin of dog food: what is life like for him? Lord, have mercy on all who live alone. And thank God for the company of pets. The trolley loaded up with drink – is that a celebration, or an addiction? Which prayer do I use? And the mother with screaming children trying to put things she doesn't want in the trolley – Lord, thank you for family life, and have mercy on parents tried beyond their limits by the demands of small children. The carer taking people with learning disabilities on their weekly shopping trip – Lord, have mercy on all who can't join fully in the life around them, and thank God for all who care for them. This is not done in any judgemental way

– looking at my own trolley will soon make me realize that I am in no superior position. Do I really need all that I have picked up, or was I seduced by the latest adverts? And did I go for the fairly traded goods, or the brands I really prefer? Lord, have mercy on me, and give me a thankful heart for all the blessings I enjoy.

Praying for the world

'God saw everything that he had made, and indeed, it was very good.' (Genesis 1.31)

I wonder what God makes of it now, when he looks at the world. Perhaps, with tears in his eyes, God says, 'What a mess.' But nothing can stop God loving his world. When we engage in intercession, we are saying to God, 'We love your world too, and we want to help you make a difference.'

We can't pray as though the world is something apart from us – we are part of the problem, as well as being potentially part of the solution. Alan Ecclestone wrote in an article about prayer[1] that everything we do, say or think is either prayer or anti-prayer. Intercession is a way of praying that expresses our intention of putting our energy alongside God's energy. We don't simply hand everything over to God for God to sort out, we offer ourselves to God to be used. Intercession is dangerous prayer, for we are quite likely to be challenged with 'What are you going to do about the situation?' We won't all be called out to the troubled spots, but we may well find ourselves being nudged into supporting those who do go. And one of the ways our intercession can be most fruitful is in asking questions of those with power – political pressure is part of this prayer.

It is important to remember those who perpetrate evil, as well as the victims. We sometimes hesitate to do that, because we think that to pray for someone somehow suggests that we are approving of their actions, or praying for their well-being. The 'evil doers' are also loved by God, and our prayer is an expression of our desire that they will know that love for themselves, and experience a change of heart and action. They are only different from us in the degree to which they give reign to their murderous desires – few of us can say that we have never had a desire to harm someone. 'Lord, have mercy' is a prayer that we all need to pray.

It is sometimes helpful to pray using a visual aid, and a physical action. A map of the world can be used in conjunction with various objects:

- Read the vision of the New Jerusalem, Revelation 22.1–2, and invite people to place a leaf on the map.
- Read Julian of Norwich's vision of the hazelnut (*Revelation of Divine Love*, Long Text ch. 5) and invite people to place a hazelnut on the map.
- Remind people that Jesus is the light of the world, and invite people to place a lit candle on the map.
- The action can be accompanied by a brief spoken prayer.
- (Reassure participants that this is not a Geography test – God understands what we want to pray for even if we are not very sure where in the world it is.)

When sufficient time has elapsed for all who want to take part to do so, draw together all the prayers, spoken aloud or inwardly, in the words of the litany which follows. The response to the petition 'Come, Lord' can be varied according to the situation. 'Let your healing power be known' is one possibility, or 'Let your love be shown'.

End the time by praying that in everything we are, or do, or say or think we may be signs of God's kingdom, as we say the Lord's Prayer together.

Note

1. In Jim Cotter, ed., *Firing the Clay*, Cairns Publications, 1999.

A litany for the world

In the places of decision-making
and the places of powerlessness:
Come, Lord . . .

In the places of wealth
and the places of poverty:
Come, Lord . . .

Where we are healthy
and where we are sick:
Come, Lord . . .

In the streets of plenty
and in the dark corners and alleys:
Come, Lord . . .

Where people are oppressed
And in the hearts of the oppressors:
Come, Lord . . .

In our places of worship
And where there is no faith:
Come, Lord . . .

In our places of learning
and in the depths of our ignorance:
Come, Lord . . .

In our homes and our welcomes
and where people couldn't care less:
Come, Lord . . .

Leading intercessions

Being asked to lead the intercessions in a service can strike terror into people's hearts! A workshop drawing on the ideas set out in the section 'Praying for the World' can offer people a chance to look at what is involved, and develop the basic skills required to encourage everyone present to pray.

As well as discussion about what we think the prayer of intercession is, it is helpful to have material for people to look at – there are many books on the market now which give ideas. And it is useful, too, to let people try out the sound system, or see how their voices work in the building used for worship.

When I run a workshop, I normally prepare intercessions for a particular occasion, usually a couple of Sundays ahead, and explain what led me to include or exclude some items which might have been appropriate. Selection is a very important principle – we can't pray for everything every week. World events and local situations can change in the time between the preparation of the prayers, and the service in which they will be used, so it is important to be able to be flexible.

I have drawn up some guidelines which can be useful as a basis for discussion and practice.

- Set the preparation in the context of your own prayer. Ask for the guidance of the Holy Spirit.
- When preparing the prayers, look at the readings and themes for the day. If possible, ask the preacher what the sermon is likely to be about. Look at parish/diocesan/circuit cycles of prayer.
- Select from all the above, and your local knowledge and awareness of what is happening in the world to decide on the areas you want to pray for.
- Look at some of the available books for ideas. You may discover helpful ways of saying things. You do not have

to use whole prayers – the odd sentence is often useful.

- When you begin to write your prayers, remember to address them to God.
- Remember to give thanks, as well as to ask.
- Remember how your sentences begin, and keep them consistent. (If you ask for God's blessing on someone or some situation, don't, within the same sentence, say *for*.)
- Keep the prayers brief – let people have time for their own thoughts and prayers.
- On the day, have a pen handy, so that you can put in last-minute requests, or respond to something the preacher has said. But don't re-preach the sermon, or try to improve on it!
- When the time comes, wait for people to settle physically, and leave a space for them to gather their thoughts.
- Speak slowly – feel that your pace is slow. Pray the prayers, rather than just saying them.
- Pause. Let spaces grow between the sentences. Give people time to respond inwardly to what you have said.
- Breathe deeply, hold your head up, and look towards the end of the place in which you are speaking. Pitch your voice low (especially women) – that way the sound carries further. Throw your voice to the end of the room.
- If you want to change the response to the petitions, make sure people know what they have to say. Instead of 'Lord, in your mercy' with the response 'Hear our prayer', you might want to say, 'Lord, hear us' with the response 'Graciously hear us'. So tell the congregation, and give them a chance to try it before you continue with the prayers. It is probably best not to change the response in the middle of the prayers.

Leading prayers is your offering to God. You don't have to worry about whether you are as good as other people – this week it's your turn. You may feel nervous, but breathing deeply as people settle down will help you to settle too. People value variety and freshness, so enjoy taking your turn.

The Bible: story and ourselves

'This year,' said a friend of mine, 'I'm going to read the Bible.'

I was rather surprised, for she had always been very scornful of religious practice. I was interested to know more.

'How are you going to set about it?' I asked.

'I'm going to start at the beginning, and read all the way through. Don't tell me it's the wrong way to do it.'

So I didn't. But I could imagine her progress, and almost predict chapter and verse where her resolution would, almost literally, run into the sand. Genesis starts off promisingly, there are some very good stories in it: the Creation, the Flood, the family sagas of Abraham, Isaac and Jacob, and the beautifully told story of Joseph. And the book of Exodus is almost as exciting as the people are freed from slavery in Egypt and journey through the desert, discovering the generous love and care God has for them. But attention begins to waver as the writer presents instructions for the building of the Tabernacle, the size of the altar, the robes for the priests. And after Exodus comes Leviticus, where you have to be really determined to stick with it as laws and rituals about things we don't usually mention in polite conversation are described in minute detail. There are more exciting stories to come, but Leviticus is probably the point at which anyone who thought the Bible was a book to read through from beginning to end would give up.

The Bible isn't a book, but a collection of books, put together at various points in the history of the people whose story it tells, and edited several times in the process. So one of the first things we need to do is to discover the context of what we are reading. (*The Lion Handbook to the Bible* is quite a good starting point.)

And it is helpful, too, to think about the nature of story. Everybody loves a good story. We probably don't remember being read to as children, but bedtime stories are part of the reassurance that everything is under control, ordered. At this point, if at no other during the day, we have someone's undivided attention; we hear a story in which frightening or evil people or powers are inevitably conquered. Stories are the stage on which our fears and terrors can be encountered, in the safe knowledge that good will win. We never tire of hearing them, and woe betide anyone who tries to skip a page.

Stories aren't just about being reassured, feeling secure in the knowledge that everything is under control. They are much more powerful. We use story to discover the roots of our history and our culture. Families bind themselves together, or sometimes destroy each other, by their stories – listen in on a gathering at a wedding or funeral! We use stories when we meet people, and talk about who they are in terms of where they've come from, and where they hope they're going.

But stories are more important even than that. They are ways of engaging our imagination, helping us to explore things about our own personalities. Fairy stories, folk tales, religious stories, biographies, even fiction (however firm the disclaimer that no living person is portrayed in the story) are all written out of experience; all alike give us a framework, a vocabulary for dealing with ideas that are perhaps too painful to deal with directly.

Stories don't necessarily illustrate, make things easy. They involve us, provoke us into response. They sneak past our defences and catch us off guard. The story of David and Bathsheba, and the way Nathan the prophet brought David to an understanding of what he had done illustrates this well (2 Samuel 11–12.14).

Apart from the fact that to have gone to the king and told him off for committing adultery and murder might have resulted in an unpleasant experience for Nathan, it would also have put David on the defensive. Telling David a story was a stroke of genius. David got so involved that he couldn't restrain his anger: 'Who is that man? He must die.'

And having made his judgement, he can't evade his own story; he takes responsibility for what he has done.

Stories may take us out of ourselves, give us a break, but they give us back to ourselves with deeper understanding, seeing more clearly where our responsibility lies, which in turn frees us from the guilt which so often prevents us from moving on in our lives. And listening to people's stories reassures us that we are not alone – there may not be an obviously happy ending, but there are companions along the way who are closer to us than perhaps we realized.

The Bible is full of stories, and they all contribute to one big story, the story of God's love affair with his people. 'You are precious in my sight, and honoured, and I love you' (Isaiah 43.4). The Bible is not a book of instructions, but an invitation to listen to God's story, which is our story too. God doesn't tell us what to think, God invites us to discover who we are as we follow the events described in the Old Testament, and respond to the challenge of the prophets who, like Nathan, brought people face to face with the consequences of their choices. And in the New Testament, we meet the Word of God in a fresh way in Jesus, and think about how we might have responded if we had been there with him. What does it mean to be precious in God's eyes? The story of Jesus tells us that it doesn't mean that we will be spoilt. Although Jesus knew himself to be loved, he was not spared the cross, or the feeling of being totally alone. But he also knew that God is faithful, and that nothing in the end will be able to separate us from God's love.

The story of God's love continues as our personal story unfolds. The challenge for us is to discover where God is in the particular circumstances of our lives, or in the world around us. The Bible can help us not so much by giving us the right answers to our questions, but by helping us to ask the right questions, and nudging us into making appropriate responses. When we read the Bible we need to ask, as happens in at least one church at the end of a reading, 'How is this the word of God for us today?'

Christmas challenge

Jesus, Bread of Life,
sleeping in a feeding trough,
in Bethlehem.
House of Bread, that's what
your name means,
Bethlehem.
You did not know then
that you sheltered bread
which would be broken
to give life to all.

Jesus, Bread of Life,
living within us, as we
feed on you, we become
bread to nourish all around.
We must be taken, blessed,
broken and shared,
channels of the eternal
Love and Life of God.[1]

Note

1. Ann Lewin, previously unpublished.

Intercessions for a Christmas Midnight Service

Glory to God in the highest, and peace to his people on earth. As we hear the angels' song, we join them in worship, and rejoice that you have come among us, Lord God, to be with us for ever. Help us to witness to that truth in our daily lives.

Lord, in your mercy:
Hear our prayer.

Lord, you came among us as Prince of Peace. We pray for peace, especially tonight in Bethlehem and the rest of the Holy Land. We pray that people of all races and creeds throughout the world will learn to live together, respecting each other, and seeking the good of all.

Lord, in your mercy:
Hear our prayer.

Lord God, you came among us as a sign of hope. We pray for all who find hope difficult to hold onto . . . refugees, asylum seekers, political prisoners, the hungry and homeless and the unloved. We thank you for those who work to make life better for others, and we pray that we will take every opportunity to help.

Lord, in your mercy:
Hear our prayer.

Lord, you came among us as light. We pray for wisdom for all in authority, that all who have power may use it with imagination and consideration for others. We pray for world leaders, and for each other in our own areas of influence and responsibility.

Lord, in your mercy:
Hear our prayer.

Lord Christ, you came that we should have fullness of life. We thank you for the life of this city, and our local community. We pray for all who are celebrating tonight in churches, pubs, clubs and at home. We pray that all of us, wherever we are, precious to you even when we don't respond to your love, will know your stillness at the heart of our festivities, and be touched by your redeeming love.

Lord, in your mercy:
Hear our prayer.

Lord, you came to bring healing and wholeness. We pray for all who suffer. As we give thanks for our families and friends, we pray for those for whom Christmas is difficult: those who will wake to another day of loneliness or pain; those whose celebration has been marred by the death of a loved one, or the disappearance of a member of their family.

In a moment of quiet, we bring our own needs into your healing presence.

Lord, in your mercy:
Hear our prayer.

Whatever lies ahead of us, may we always hear the echo of the angels' song, and help others to hear it too.

Merciful Father, accept these prayers for the sake of your Son, our Saviour Jesus Christ. **Amen.**

At the turn of the year

'New beginnings are always delightful, the threshold is the place to pause.' So said Robert Louis Stevenson. I'm not sure I fully agree with him. New beginnings, full of promise though they may be, are often close to endings which may have been painful. New beginnings always mean change, and there is something in all of us that makes us want to hold on to old, familiar, comfortable things. There may be quite a few of us who were given new slippers for Christmas, who are keeping them for best for the time being – they're too good for doing the housework or the gardening in: thinly disguised excuses for hanging on to the old.

But the threshold is the place to pause, yes. Thresholds are places of promise. In biblical terms they mark off something holy, a place where God is. We stand at the beginning of a year, a year where we shall find God. We don't have to take God with us into the new year, God takes us with him. That's what Christmas is about. Emmanuel, God with us. We don't have to cling on to Christmas, for Christmas is never over, God is with us.

Just before Christmas, the children came forward at the end of one service to report on their morning's activities. They had been thinking about the Christmas story, and some of the words it introduces us to. One of the words was 'Emmanuel'.

'What does that word mean?' asked the vicar.

There was a long pause, then a little boy said, 'I love you.'

That's not the official theologian's answer, but he'd gone right to the heart of it. 'I love you.' What we take with us into the new year, as reassurance and also as challenge, is the unfailing love of God. God's love isn't always comfortable. It doesn't always make things right for us. It doesn't mean we won't suffer, or find the world a difficult place to live in. God's love means that God is with us, right in the pain and the mess as well as the joy and the laughter. Christmas will never be over, it is always just beginning.

Pause at the threshold, and remember that God's love is new every morning: words worth pondering daily as we discover the riches and marvels of that love.

Epiphany

Picture the scene: a room with a large dining table. Three men in sumptuous flowing robes are watching a fourth man, obviously a servant, laying the table. Through a window, which by its shape tells us that this is a scene from the East, you can see a couple approaching in the distance, pushing a buggy with a child in it. One of the men explains the situation to the servant, who is looking a bit puzzled: 'You see, last year we went to them, so this year they are coming to us.'

I admire the skill of cartoonists, who with a few strokes of the pen and some well-chosen words can make a comment about our human condition, and at the same time make us think about deeper truths.

Over the last few years, cartoonists have provided some interesting springboards for thought about this Epiphany story. The one I have just described latches on to a perennial anxiety about where parts of a family spend Christmas, and whose turn it is to be host. With luck, we can laugh about it. But the deep truth about Jesus spending Christmas with us is that he comes every year, and stays with us all the time. So the real question is not about whose turn it is, but about how we are going to respond to this amazing generosity of God in giving himself to us.

The Wise Men in the story responded by offering gifts to the Christ-child. Another cartoon shows them having a conversation with each other. Two of them are holding the traditional gifts, the third is holding an envelope. In response to their concerned looks, he says, 'Yes, I know. But a token is so much lighter.' Will our response to God be a token gesture? Or will we offer something precious? And what precious thing have we got anyway? We need to be wary about using this story as if it's a prelude to a stewardship campaign – dig a little deeper into your pocket. It's more profound than that. The most precious thing we have is our-self. That is what God longs for us to give him.

We perhaps don't always think of ourselves as precious: we are quite good at putting ourselves down. But the gifts the Wise Men brought are our gifts too. Each of us is precious to God – in God's eyes each of us is pure gold. We may have to dig deep to find it, but that is God's truth about each one of us. Offer the frankincense of worship, and as we attend prayerfully to God, and learn more about God and ourselves, we recognize God's truth about us: 'You are precious in my sight, and honoured, and I love you' (Isaiah 43.4).

That truth about being precious will be tested with the myrrh of suffering – all around us, and perhaps touching us more personally too. Faithfulness to God's love is part of our response. As the carol puts it:

What can I give him,
  Poor as I am?
If I were a shepherd
  I would bring a lamb;
If I were a wise man
  I would do my part;
Yet what I can I give him –
  Give my heart.

That is a response to God not just for Epiphany, but for every day. Another cartoon takes us into the vestry, where the vicar is holding open a cupboard door. At his feet, the tiny crib figures process past him and the caption reads, 'So it was back into the vestry cupboard for another year.'

Will that be how we deal with Christmas too? Has the celebration made any difference to us? The commercial world has moved on, Christmas has been put away, hot cross buns are on sale. But Christmas isn't over. God is with us every day, the baby grows into adulthood if we will let him, and he challenges us to recognize him and respond to him in our daily lives.

Eucharistic Prayer for Epiphany

(The words at the Sanctus and at the end of the prayer come from the hymn 'Holy, holy, holy is the Lord')

Father of all blessings, we give you thanks and praise
for Jesus the Light of the world, the light that
no darkness can overpower;
we thank you that you have called us from darkness
to walk in his light;
we thank you for the insight of the Wise Men,
who by their gifts showed us
that all life is gift;
with them, and angels and archangels
and all who live in light,
we praise you, singing:
Holy, holy, holy is the Lord,
holy is the Lord God almighty, *(repeat)*
who was, and is, and is to come,
holy, holy, holy is the Lord.

Accept our praises now, Lord God,
as we remember Jesus,
who, on the night before he died,
took bread and wine, gave you thanks
and offered them to his friends, saying,
'This is my body, this is my blood.
Eat and drink to remember me.'

Come freshly to us now, Lord God,
as we offer you our lives.
Renew in us your gifts:
the gold of our potential,
the incense of our prayers and aspirations,
the myrrh of healing for our pain;
feed us and nourish us,
that we may grow in the life of Christ;

fill us with your Spirit
that we may overflow with your love,
and transform the world with your glory:
Glory, glory, glory to the Lord,
glory to the Lord God almighty, *(repeat)*
who was, and is, and is to come,
glory, glory, glory to the Lord.

The week of Prayer for Christian Unity

We have perhaps become a little stale in our observance of this week. Twenty five years ago we were often rather suspicious of each other. Some of us would never even have entered each other's churches. But there was a growing feeling that if we were to witness effectively in the world, Christians needed to present the gospel together. Many churches entered into Local Covenants, as a sign of commitment to learning to know each other and work and witness and worship together. What follows is an account of the beginnings of one such Local Covenant, which might form a focus for a review of how churches have progressed in other areas, and form a springboard for renewed effort. This Covenant was made between Roman Catholic, Methodist, Anglican and Baptist churches.

As people came into the Baptist Church, where the chairs were arranged in the round, they found the circle divided by a wall of cardboard boxes, labelled with words identifying divisions between the churches, such as priesthood, authority, free prayer, abortion, infallibility, ordination of women, infant baptism . . .

The explanation of the wall

Since time began, people have built walls: to defend their territory, to protect their property, to exclude others, to give themselves security. Church people are no exceptions – from being people who were remarked on as having all things in common, we developed through the ages into groups which excluded each other from Communion, and denied each other's integrity. Our wall is built of deeply held beliefs, deeply rooted prejudices, half understood fears, inherited misunderstandings. From where you sit, some of the obstacles seem insuperable. From your neighbour's angle they may appear to be trivial, irritating stumbling blocks.

At times, the wall has been so high that it was impossible to see over it. Those on our side seemed to be the only ones who believed the truth. More recently, the wall has begun to crumble. We have seen that there are people outside our own tradition who are very like us in belief and practice. They even now talk something like the same language. Occasional forays over the wall have taught us that we are not so very different, and even if we don't feel that the grass is greener, at least we have discovered that it tastes remarkably similar. Here our wall is quite low, but it is still there. Some of the beliefs and practices it symbolizes will not yield easily to our attempts to understand and appreciate them. Some will never be congenial to our different tastes. But tonight, in coming to sign this covenant we are coming to offer to God not only our desire for deeper unity, but also our fears and hesitations and our unwillingness to change. We are going to proclaim again our belief that God can and does use the raw material of our lives and transform it into the means that he will use to redeem the world.

We are going, symbolically, to turn our wall into a Cross, and we shall see that the things that divide us are also the things that in Christ will unite us. And in the centre of the Cross is the focus of our activity tonight.

At this point, representatives of each of the participating churches moved the top layer of boxes from the wall, and placed them to form the arms of the Cross, with the table at which the Local Covenant was to be signed at the centre.

We have moved on from those days. Real friendships have been made across the denominational edges. People now are much more accepting of each other's different ways of understanding their faith, and of their different practices. We have begun to work together in our local communities. But we are still divided.

Michael Lloyd, in *Café Theology* says:

> The cross is the great act of wall demolition. The church is to be the community that lives in defiance of the walls that divide our world, not the community that erects more of its own. If I were an atheist attempting to demonstrate the falsity of the Christian faith, I would not take my stand on the problem of evil, nor would I focus on the historical basis of the Christian faith. No, I would concentrate my fire on the disunity of the church. Here is far more fruitful territory . . . The cross is supposed to have broken these barriers down. The church is meant to be the new society living across the divides that riddle the rest of humanity. But the church is as riddled with division as the rest of the world. It is to my mind the one nearly unanswerable argument against the truth of the gospel.[1]

He goes on to say: 'We need to make every effort, not just to maintain the unity of the Spirit, but to recover it and to live it. We need to help the world to believe by living out the unity that proclaims there is one God. It is an evangelistic imperative as well as a matter of integrity.'

Robert Frost in his poem 'Mending Wall' says:

> Before I built a wall I'd ask to know
> What I was walling in or walling out,
> And to whom I was like to give offence.
> Something there is that doesn't love a wall,
> That wants it down.[2]

Another American poet, Edwin Markham, wrote:

> He drew a circle that shut me out –
> Heretic, rebel, a thing to flout.
> But Love and I had the wit to win:
> We drew a circle that took him in.[3]

In a review of growth in unity, it might be helpful to ponder these questions:

1. If you had a wall like the one described above, how would you label the boxes in your own area?
2. What steps have you taken in your area to break down barriers?
3. What would help you to be more effective in mission?

Looking to the future, we might ask, how has the life of churches in the area changed? Who else might be drawn into closer fellowship? We have a call to mission, set out in 1 Peter 2, 4–5, and 9

> Come to him, a living stone, though rejected by mortals, yet chosen and precious in God's sight, and like living stones let yourselves be built into a spiritual house, to be a holy priesthood.
> 9. You are a chosen race, a royal priesthood, a holy nation, God's own people, in order that you may proclaim the mighty acts of him who called you out of darkness into his marvelous light.

What kind of wall might we build now?

Questions to ponder

1. What gifts do you bring to your wall of living stones?
2. What is the purpose of your wall?
3. What help do you need to build it to God's design?

Notes

1. Michael Lloyd, *Café Theology*, Alpha International, 2005.
2. Robert Frost, 'Mending Wall', *North of Boston*, Henry Holt and Co., 1915.
3. Edwin Markham, 'Outwitted', *The Shoes of Happiness and Other Poems*, University of Michigan Press, 1915.

Candlemas – the Presentation of Christ in the Temple

The story of the Presentation of Christ told in Luke's Gospel (Luke 2.22–38), is one in which Anna and Simeon have a senior moment to die for – they are privileged to see the one who is to be the Saviour of the world.

Usually when we talk about having a senior moment, it's a rather rueful reference to memory failure. It's one of the kinder ways in which we refer to the business of growing older. Our society isn't always as kind when old age is under discussion. There are hints that old people pose a problem: pension funds won't last because old people are living longer; there are concerns about funding care for those who are unable to look after themselves, or finding people to do the caring.

This gospel story is about two old people who show some of the positive attributes of old age. They represent wisdom and simplicity, and offer us some helpful ideas about using our later years.

First, it's worth thinking about wisdom. There are others in the Christmas story, those visitors from the East who play a much more prominent part, whom we call wise. But a more accurate name for the Wise Men is 'Magi', marking them out as scientists of their time, discovering the secrets of the stars. Their 'wisdom' was perhaps more the cleverness of people who had a lot of knowledge in their heads, rather than the wisdom of the heart which brings insight into human behaviour. When you think about it, the Magi caused quite a lot of trouble with their cleverness, by jumping to conclusions about where the one who was to be the King of the Jews would be found. It's reasonable to think first of the ruler's palace: but such a birth would only be the cause of rejoicing if the child were the first-born. Herod already had a family which was torn apart by jealousies and intrigues.

If the Magi had researched more widely, they would have discovered how much the Jews hated Herod and all he stood for. Then they might have approached their search for the new-born king rather differently, and avoided the problem that Herod could only deal with by murder. It wasn't very clever, let alone wise, to go to Herod.

Matthew was not writing his Gospel to comment on the Magi's method of discovery, but to show how Old Testament prophecies about the Messiah coming for all nations were fulfilled by their arrival to pay homage. Luke makes the same point about the Messiah being for all, when Simeon, in his recognition of Jesus, speaks of him in words that echo a prophecy of Isaiah: a light to lighten the Gentiles, as well as being the glory of God's people, Israel (Isaiah 49.6).

Simeon and Anna display the wisdom which begins with attentiveness to God and God's word. 'The fear of the Lord is the beginning of wisdom' (Ecclesiasticus 1.14).

'Fear', not in the sense of being afraid, but having a proper respect and reverence. Simeon and Anna recognize the significance of what is going on around them because they had waited, alert and hopeful, for the fulfilment of their longing. *Their* longing belonged to their circumstances, people of God oppressed, as they saw it, by a foreign power, longing for the promised Saviour who would set them free. They were not put off by the setbacks their people had experienced – they kept their vision alive, trusting that God would not let them down. They gave practical expression to their hope by being faithful to their religious observance. So they were there when Mary and Joseph brought Jesus to the Temple, and they had eyes to see the promise in this child. They were realistic enough also to say that there would be no easy ride for child or parents in bringing that promise to fruition. I'm sure Mary remembered Simeon's words about a sword piercing her soul, as she watched her son grow up.

Simeon and Anna were old, and probably in the eyes of those around didn't achieve very much. But age isn't a time for productivity, it's the time for fruitfulness, a much longer-term result of growth. It's the stage when the wisdom we have acquired over the years can be harvested and shared.

Wisdom begins with attentiveness to God in prayer and worship, and alertness to the signs of God's coming in daily life. And wisdom grows when we give ourselves time to reflect, and give God a chance to reveal truth to us. Simeon and Anna took time – time to stand on the edge of the mystery of life and wonder at it, just as children do. Jesus said we need to become like children. People often talk about second childhood as a time of diminishment, and sadly, in our imperfect world, it can be. But let's not forget the good things about having a childlike attitude – perhaps the fact that grandparents and grandchildren enjoy life together can teach us something about that kind of simplicity.

So, time to explore the mystery of life, and time to explore the mystery of God. People used to talk about 'making their soul' in the last stages of life – learning to pray, to love, to be content, to enjoy beauty. We may not understand the mystery any more clearly, or find the answers to all our questions. But we may find that some of our questions don't matter all that much in the end. All that matters is that we are loved by God with a love that never fails. That's not to deny the difficulties and challenges of life, but to take hold of a very important resource our faith gives: 'It is better to light a candle', as the Chinese proverb puts it, 'than to curse the darkness'.

Age does not have to mean diminishment. There may well be constraints: stiff joints, failing sight, a less reliable memory. There will be things we have to let go of – not always easy. And the last letting go happens when we die. Our society regards death as a failure, something to be avoided at all costs. But we can't avoid it for ever: and Christians have something very important to say about death. Perhaps we could begin to think about death as the last gift God will give us in this life, the gift that will take us into his fuller presence. Simeon seems to have felt something of that – he was ready to die. We don't know whether he died that day, or after an interval. We don't have to go out and seek death

– but we do need to think about it, and learn that God's love will hold us through that experience too.

Candlemas is sometimes spoken of as the day when the Church's year changes direction. We stop looking back to Christmas, and begin to look forward to Lent and Good Friday and Easter. It's the growing time of the year, a season that will offer us plenty of opportunity to practise and grow in wisdom, so that, like Anna and Simeon, we recognize the moments of God's coming, and rejoice in God's love every day.

Eucharistic Prayer for Candlemas

Father of light, we give you thanks and praise
through Jesus Christ your Son, our Lord,
the light of the world
which no darkness can overcome.
We praise you that you have called us
from darkness to live in Christ's light.
With angels and archangels,
and all who are in that light, we praise you, singing:
Holy, holy, holy Lord,
God of light and love,
heaven and earth are full of your glory,
all praise to your name.

Come freshly to us now, Lord God.
Kindle again the light of your love
in our hearts, as we remember Jesus,
who, on the night before he died,
took bread and wine, blessed them
and gave them to his friends, saying,
'This is my body, this is my blood.
Eat and drink to remember me.'

Pour out your Holy Spirit, Lord,
set us on fire,
burn from us all that dims your light;
kindle an answering flame in lives around,
that darkness may be driven back,
and the whole world
come to live in your light.
For you are the God in whom is no darkness.
To you be praise and glory for ever. **Amen.**

Section 2

Lent to Pentecost

Thinking about Lent

> 'Most people think that behaviour matters and prayer helps it. The truth is that prayer matters, and behaviour tests it.' (Archbishop William Temple)[1]

Fifty years or so ago, at each of the weekly confirmation classes I attended, the vicar read some verses from Philippians 3. In the Authorised Version, just about the only version available at the time, the words weren't very exciting. But they stayed with me, surfacing from time to time, and coming to life anew as different NT translations appeared: 'I want to know Christ and the power of his resurrection' (Philippians 3.10). On good days, when I'm asked what I really, really want, I know that's my answer: to know Christ, to be open to receive the gift of the risen life, to live it to God's glory and the benefit of my fellow humans.

Not all days are like that, though. There are all kinds of things that distract me from that focus. Paul knew about that too, and wrote about our need for discipline as an athlete needs to keep in training. Lent comes as a timely reminder, so I shall select one of my self-indulgences and attempt to show it who's mistress. But Lent isn't primarily a time for self-improvement, although that may be a spin-off. It is a time to grow, and my real aim, as it has been for some years, is to *do* less, and to *be* more; to spend more time doing nothing, being still, listening, looking, waiting in expectancy for God. And that kind of prayerfulness doesn't only operate in the times we label prayer, nor does it stop with the end of Lent, but grows in the whole of life, through Easter and beyond. It's another way of expressing what the Benedictines call conversion of life: a steady, continual turning to focus on God, opening up to God's Spirit, so that Christ can live his risen life in us.

Quite a challenge. And responding to it will keep me going for the rest of my life, let alone my Lents. But Lent comes to remind us to make space, paradoxically, to work at doing nothing, to make ourselves available to receive God's gift of life. For it is all gift. The risen life is not something I can achieve by my efforts, nor is it something I can do better than anyone else. We are not in competition over this, as we sometimes are over our Lenten discipline (is it more merit-worthy to give up chocolate or alcohol?). Receiving the gift of life means letting God free me to be 'God's work of art' (another phrase from Paul in Ephesians 2.10, brought to life this time by the Jerusalem Bible); it is coming to know deep down that I am precious in God's sight, and honoured, and loved (Isaiah 43.4). My response will be tested out in engagement with life, as I seek to enable others to receive God's gift, with all that implies of involvement with issues of social concern.

For me the question is not so much how I can best use Lent, but how I can best let God use it in me.

Note

1. See note 1 to 'Thinking About Prayer' in Section 1, p. 15.

At a Eucharist with the Imposition of Ashes on Ash Wednesday

Readings: Isaiah 58.1–12; Matthew 6.1–8

Growing in love – that's the aim of all our discipline and study during Lent. In this service we hear a lot about penitence, and our need to recall our commitment. We may well have decided on some form of discipline to remind us of that commitment. But our readings have reminded us that religious practice is nothing if it doesn't go any deeper than pious acts. The point of the practice is to draw us more deeply into love for God and our neighbour.

St Matthew records Jesus telling people that they are not in a religious competition to demonstrate how holy they are. Prayer, fasting, almsgiving are not to be engaged in to impress the neighbours, either in church or outside it. If we aim for that, we might get that as our reward. But it won't cut much ice with God. Prayer, fasting, almsgiving are to be signs of our desire to love God by deepening our relationship with God, being single-minded in our service of God, and generous in sharing what God gives us with others. Isaiah set out a concept of fasting which involved tackling oppression, hunger, homelessness and poverty. That's what pleases God, he said, not a lot of outwardly pious actions. Both these readings recall us to the basic demands of the Commandments, which are to love God and our neighbour.

That's what we all want to do. But we don't always manage it. We get deflected, distracted . . . it's the story of our life. And the symbolism of this service is the story of our life too. We are invited to receive the sign of the cross in ash on our foreheads. We are recalled to our baptismal vows, when the sign of the cross was first placed on us, vows made for most of us by parents and godparents, but made our own at confirmation: vows about turning away from sin and following Christ. The sign will be made in the same place as on that first occasion. It will be made in ash, which traditionally is obtained by burning the palm crosses we received last year. By accepting them, we said that we were willing to take up our cross and be faithful to Christ. The palm crosses have been burnt as a reminder that we have failed, been distracted, forgotten our calling.

We are called to penitence, which is not grovelling about how awful we are, but an acknowledgement that for all our desire to be faithful, we are often anything but. It isn't only the things we do or don't do that we have to recognize: those sins of commission and omission. There are the sins of permission too, the things we allow to happen because we can't summon the energy or courage to challenge them. Failure to love our neighbour often comes into this category.

Penitence should never leave us thinking about ourselves, for it turns us to God who meets us with love. Our response is thankfulness for God's forgiveness and grace. Penitence is the beginning of repentance, the continual turning back to God whenever we find that we have turned away. It's part of the process of learning to be faithful. We can't do it on our own, but God believes in us, and gives us his life continually. 'God's holy gifts for God's holy people', we hear at the Eucharist. That's who we are, deep down, but we have to become that every day. In Lent we symbolize that by some kind of discipline, not so that we can be proud of ourselves at the end of Lent, because we haven't indulged in whatever it is we have chosen to give up, but to remind ourselves of our need for God, to let God feed us with himself. And we may not find ourselves giving up consumables: we may decide that the discipline we need is to express our love for our neighbours in practical ways. Caring for the hungry, the homeless, the oppressed, the poor – all those spring from the love God gives us too.

Feeding on God by faith with thanksgiving – that's what makes Lent fruitful – a veritable feast. George Herbert began one of his poems, 'Welcome deare feaste of Lent'. We fast so that we have space to feast on the goodness of God. Lent isn't a spiritual endurance test, it's the springtime of our spiritual lives, when we clear out the clutter and re-focus on God. And we begin by responding to God's call, 'Turn away from sin, and follow Christ.'

The experience of receiving the mark of ash is liberating:

Ashing

Light as a feather
A finger touched me,
Branded me cross-shaped,
Smudged me with ash.

Light as a feather
God's finger caressed me
With sign of forgiveness,
Marked me with love.

Light as a feather,
Penitent, shriven,
Signed with his life-mark
I go on my way.[1]

May that be our experience as we grow in grace and love this Lent.

Note

1. *Watching for the Kingfisher*, p. 80.

Eucharistic Prayer for Lent

Lord God,
you fill us with longing for your presence,
yet require us to live with a sense of your absence.
Open our ears to hear the echo of your praise,
and tune our voices to sing your song,
as with angels and archangels,
and people of faith on different paths, we sing:
Holy, holy, holy Lord
God of life and love,
heaven and earth are full of your glory,
all praise to your name.

Come to us now, Lord God,
as we remember Jesus, who,
on the night before he died,
took bread and wine, blessed them
and gave them to his friends, saying,
'This is my body, this is my blood.
Eat and drink to remember me.'

Lord God, you have drawn us together
on the way of the cross,
and illumined our path
by the insights of others;
Come freshly to us, loving God,
with your disturbing power;
and as we receive this gift
of the life of your Son,
give us the courage to stay with
the discomfort of your call, and
satisfy our longing to be
in harmony with your will.

Draw us to deeper commitment
to each other and to you,
that we may live to your glory
and sing to your praise all our days. Amen.

Mothering Sunday – say it with flowers

Mothering Sunday is a good occasion to think about the nature of God – for, as Julian of Norwich said in the fourteenth century, 'as truly as God is our Father, so also is God our Mother'.

People sometimes think that feminine imagery for God is very new, but it goes way back to some of the early books of the Bible. What about 'The eternal God is your refuge, and underneath are the everlasting arms' (Deuteronomy 33.27 NIV), or 'Can a woman forget her nursing child, or show no compassion for the child of her womb?' (Isaiah 49.15)? The prophet Hosea described the way God cared for his people in a very maternal way. 'It was I who taught Ephraim to walk, I took them up in my arms, but they did not know that I healed them. I led them with cords of human kindness, with the bands of love. I was to them like those who lift infants to their cheeks. I bent down to them and fed them' (Hosea 11.3–4).

We don't have to start calling God 'Mother' – that isn't necessarily any more helpful than 'Father'. But it is worth noting that there is this element in the biblical tradition, and it has been picked up by people in the centuries since.

So how can we respond to this God who is mother and father and so much else besides? Today, perhaps, we could say it with flowers.

How on earth can we do that? No floral delivery system has a way to cope with it! But we do talk about offering ourselves to God. I don't suppose you have ever thought of yourself as a flower, even though flower allusions abound in our language: we talk about being as 'fresh as a daisy', or we describe someone as being 'a shrinking violet'. People are sometimes 'prickly'.

But when you think about it, what kind of flower are you? Are you like a camellia, rather startlingly beautiful? Or like rosemary, starting to bloom right at the beginning of your life, and continuing year on year? Are you one of those plants that doesn't flower often? Or one that props others up? Are you a plant with rather insignificant flowers, but always there in the background to help others give of their best? Do you fill the world with fragrance, or give flavour to life?

Are you one of the plants that bring hope in the dark days of winter? Some plants are very beautiful when their flowers are dead – some people come into their own at the end of their life.

Sometimes we put a single flower into a vase and enjoy its beauty. At other times, we put many different varieties together in an arrangement. There is an important place for our individual response to God, but when we come together as a church we discover new things about ourselves as we relate to each other as well as to God. Like a flower arrangement, we can bring out the best in each other, and complement and support each other.

On our own perhaps we don't look very exciting – that doesn't mean we don't have our own beauty – but put with others, the ones who are a bit shy can find support, and those who are rather exotic can lend their colour and perfume to the more retiring. Even those who are prickly can be a great support to those who are fragile.

So we can give God quite a bouquet – and if we listen carefully, we'll hear God say, as every mother does, 'Thank you, dear, that's lovely!'

(One way of developing this idea is to accompany the words with some flower arranging, or to produce an arrangement that has been prepared earlier. This can be incorporated into the offertory. In one church, at the end of the service, the arrangement was given to the vicar, so that he could enjoy it during the week, and pray for his people too. The idea has also been used in one session of a Quiet Day. It could be followed by a session on being chosen. See the Quiet Day material in Section 3, pp. 178–182.)

Palm Sunday

I wonder what the donkey made of it all? Donkeys play quite a significant part in the stories of the Bible. They do the donkey-work, quite literally, and they were highly prized, especially the females. I don't think they were ever sacrificed – perhaps they were more valuable alive. For example, there was a donkey who spoke: Balaam's ass. She saw what was going on – more than the boss did, in fact, and eventually spoke to draw his attention to the presence of an angel. (Read her story in Numbers 22–24.) A donkey also carried Jesus invisibly to Bethlehem – perhaps he was present at his birth?

Another donkey, today's, carried Jesus publicly into Jerusalem. I wonder where she was at the end of the week. Was she tethered somewhere near the cross, with her foal? Why remember all these donkeys? I want to suggest that we are very like them. No offence! I don't just mean that we share their stubbornness and need a lot of coaxing sometimes; or that we always get lumbered with the donkey-work; or that we all behave like silly asses sometimes. All these are true in some measure. But we share something else that is much more important. Nearly all donkeys bear the mark of a cross on their backs. We carry the mark of the cross too, given us in baptism.

So what do these donkeys tell us about discipleship?

They remind us that we always carry Jesus invisibly, like Mary's donkey, wherever we go. Every day Christ is carried into his city, into his world, by us. As St Theresa said, 'Christ has no body now on earth but ours, no hands but ours, no feet but ours. Ours are the feet on which he is to go about doing good, ours the eyes through which he is to look with compassion on the world, ours the hands with which he is to bless us now.' So on the days when we feel we're carrying the world on our shoulders, we need to remember that we are also bearing Christ to meet the world's pain and give people life.

There are times when, like Balaam's ass, we shall see things that others can't or won't see. Then we have to do something about it. Balaam's ass tried first of all to draw the boss's attention to the demands of God, the angel standing in the way, and got pretty rough treatment for her trouble. But then God gave her words to say, and Balaam began to take God seriously.

Being a Christian, being outspoken for God, isn't always going to be easy or pleasant. Balaam was trying to maintain his reputation, and wasn't keen on anything standing in his way. We shall find ourselves challenging important people and vested interests – that can be very hard, like crucifixion.

Today's donkey reminds us that when we go with Christ, there are no promises about easy rides. We know, however, which she did not, that at the end of the suffering, after the death, there was resurrection. We know that Christ has promised to keep us company, but as we carry him with us in the world, he won't avoid confrontation, or allow us to. 'In the world', he said, 'you will have tribulation.' We know that, from personal experience, and from sharing in the pain of the world, as people starve, exploit and kill each other. We shall have to hang on with some of the donkey's stubbornness to the belief that Christ really has overcome the evil in the world, and that we shall share that victory.

So here we are, at the beginning of Holy Week, armed with our crosses, ready to ride out again with Jesus, to be his donkeys as he goes the way of his cross. God grant that we will be faithful, so that, accompanying him to the cross, we may also know in ourselves the power of his resurrection.

The Stations of the Cross

1 Jesus is condemned to death

Pilate had given in to a shouting mob before. When he took up his post, he marched into Jerusalem with the Roman Standard leading the way, and there was a riot, only quelled when the offending symbols were removed. So he'd been careful ever since not to upset the Jewish people. Tonight, faced with another mob shouting that if he let this man go he was not Caesar's friend, his blood ran cold. Torn between condemning a man he believed to be innocent, and saving his own skin, his courage failed, and he gave in. But washing his hands didn't remove his responsibility.

We pray for all innocent victims of injustice, and for all who want to act justly but fear the personal consequences.

Kyrie eleison

2 Jesus accepts his cross

This was where the buck stopped. Jesus had made the agonizing decision in the Garden of Gethsemane to do his Father's will, even though it must have been obvious to him that this would involve suffering. We need to take the long view about the nature of the will of God. God's will is that all people should be rescued from the power of sin, the apparently endless cycle of recrimination, the desire to get our own way no matter who gets hurt. Jesus accepted the Cross, refused to fight against it, and by doing so gave us encouragement to stop evil in its tracks by refusing to give as bad as we get.

We give thanks for the forgiveness we have received, from God and from the people we have hurt. We pray that nations and individuals may have the grace to be forgiving in our relationships, so that God's will may be done.

Kyrie eleison

3 Jesus falls for the first time

It was not surprising that Jesus should find the weight of the Cross unbearable. At a physical level he'd been cruelly beaten up during the night, interrogated without mercy, mocked and manhandled. But there was more to it than that. He knew that he was bearing the weight of humanity's inhumanity, bringing it all into the embrace of God's will. Humanly speaking, it was more than he could carry, and he fell.

We pray for all who suffer inhuman treatment at the hands of their fellows, whether it is physical torture or bullying of a more subtle nature. We pray that they will have strength to bear it.

We pray for all who oppress others, that they will be touched by your love and compassion. May we all learn to honour one another, and seek the common good.

Kyrie eleison

4 Jesus meets his mother

What a dreadful time this was for Mary. She had been warned right at the beginning that Jesus' life would not be easy – a child set for the fall and rising again of many in Israel, a sign that would be spoken against. She had been told that a sword would pierce her soul – and there had been many moments when she must have wondered whether she would ever understand him. But this was worse than anything else, to see her son being treated so badly, to know that he was on the way to his death, and not to be able to do anything about it. Mary is often portrayed in serene, beautiful images. Perhaps today her face would look more like those ravaged faces we see on our screens, of mothers weeping inconsolably for their dead sons and daughters.

We pray for parents who have lost their children, through illness, war or natural disaster. Lord, enfold them in your loving care.

Kyrie eleison

5 Simon of Cyrene helps Jesus carry the cross

He didn't volunteer for this. It was probably the last thing he had on his mind – in fact he was going the other way into Jerusalem, when he met this sorry procession on the way to the place of crucifixion. He had no choice when he was ordered to help carry the cross. But it proved to be a turning point in more ways than one for him. Whatever his allegiance before, he became one of Jesus' followers, and his sons Alexander and Rufus were well known in the Christian community too. Sometimes unexpected demands on us prove to have a life-giving outcome.

We pray for all at turning points in their lives. And we pray that we may all keep turning back to faithful witness to the cross which was signed on our foreheads at baptism.

Kyrie eleison

6 Veronica wipes the face of Jesus

'True icon', her name means. By tradition, Veronica received the imprint of Jesus' face on the veil with which she wiped his face as he passed her with his cross. But, like all of us, she already bore his image. In the beginning, God made us in his likeness. Our reflection of God's image has become distorted through the choices we make to follow our own will rather than God's. But when we turn again to God, through his grace, by degrees, we are changed into his likeness again.

Father, transform us by the riches of your grace.

Kyrie eleison

7 Jesus falls for the second time

A shaft of sunlight falling on a crucifix started a train of thought:

His bloodied knees
Caught my attention . . .

I've grown accustomed
To the sight of blood
Pouring from thorn-crowned head
And marks of nails and spear:
The crucified Christ
Bearing the sins of the world.
A distant Christ, carrying
The big sins – murder,
Premeditated cruelty –
Other people's sins, not often mine.
(Although I have it in me.)

But the sore knees
Brought him close.
That blood comes from
Everyone's experience.
Tripped up by inattention,
Undue haste, or thoughtlessness,
We feel the sting.
Those sins I know,
Catching me unaware.

It was the weight of such sins
Caused him to fall under the cross
And graze his knees.

Should I not then cry, Mercy?[1]

Kyrie eleison

8 Jesus meets the women of Jerusalem

There were crowds of people around, some, no doubt, there for the spectacle. But the women were anticipating his death, and mourning his fate. Jesus, in the midst of his pain, tells them that worse will follow, and that their weeping should be directed to those who will wish they had never been born.

There are plenty of reasons to weep now for what is going on in Jerusalem. We pray for peace and justice for the people of Jerusalem and the whole of the Middle East.

Kyrie eleison

9 Jesus falls for the third time

There's something about going down for the third time – death is now inevitable. Jesus had accepted the cross, and he is committed to seeing things through. He will face taunts about his apparent powerlessness when he is on the cross: 'If you are the Son of God, save yourself and us', one of the thieves will say. But Jesus shows his strength by struggling on in the midst of his pain.

We pray for all who are facing death, especially those who are alone and fearful. May we all, when our turn comes, remember that we have been given life through the mystery of Christ's death.

Kyrie eleison

10 Jesus is stripped of his garments

We never portray this exposure of Jesus in art or sculpture. For the Jews of Jesus' time, nakedness was shameful, and we haven't moved very far from that attitude in the intervening centuries. For all the flaunting of flesh in top-shelf magazines and adverts, in general we observe the decencies, as we say. So the crucified Lord is treated by us with a respect that he was certainly not given at the time. Let's not forget though, that he was subjected to this degradation.

We pray for all who are exploited physically and sexually in our own day, for all whose humanity is denied in order to satisfy the sadistic and voyeuristic desires of others.

Kyrie eleison

11 Jesus is nailed to the cross

Blows thud through him, wringing from him cries of pain and desolation. 'Why, God, why?' But even in the midst of that, Jesus never loses his concern for others. 'Father, forgive them, they don't know what they are doing.'

Things are happening at different levels. At one level, it's just another crucifixion. At another a great cosmic battle is being fought between the forces of good and evil. The two thieves exemplify that: one wants to blame Jesus for their suffering; the other wins assurance of eternal life by recognizing Jesus as a man doing something extraordinary, 'Lord, remember me when you come into your Kingdom.'

Lord we pray that we will learn to look below the outward circumstances of our lives, to discern your work of transforming us into people who bear your image ever more clearly.

Kyrie eleison

12 Jesus dies on the cross

With that great cry, 'It is finished', Jesus died. People will have heard that in different ways. For the soldiers it would have been a welcome sign that they would soon be able to go off duty, another crucifixion over. For Mary and John and Mary Magdalene, and any other of Jesus' followers who were within earshot, it would have confirmed what they feared: it was all over. All their dreams of God's Kingdom being set up on earth had become the nightmare of present experience. But for Jesus it was a cry of triumph: 'I have accomplished what I set out to do. I have met evil with love, and love has won.'

We adore you, O Christ, and we bless you, because by your cross and passion you have redeemed the world.

Kyrie eleison

13 The body of Jesus is taken down from the cross

For those who took his body down, it was a dead weight, and perhaps it seemed a dead loss. They didn't know the end of the story – in fact they thought it was the end. But we believe it was the beginning.

Lord, we pray for all who live in darkness and despair; for all who fear that death is the end; for all who dare not hope. O Light that darkness cannot extinguish, shine in our hearts and give us courage.

Kyrie eleison

14 Jesus is laid in the tomb

Jesus, his tormented body at peace, is laid in the tomb by two influential men who were generous in the extreme in their provision for his burial.

And there we leave Jesus. Again, perhaps things are not quite what they seem – Jesus' work continues as he descends into hell and rescues those still held in death's thrall. But, outwardly, his work on earth is complete, and we are invited to take into ourselves the riches of his love.

Lord Christ, call us who long to love and serve you
along the way of your Cross;
set us free from all that holds us back
with the forgiveness of your Cross;
strengthen us to be faithful
with the power of your Cross;
and bring us at last to know
the glory of your Cross.
We ask this in your name.
Amen.

Note

1. 'For my Salvation', in *Watching for the Kingfisher*, p. 56.

Maundy Thursday

Throughout the Christian world, on this day, people will be having their feet washed, re-enacting what Jesus did with his disciples the night before he was crucified. And all of them, I expect, will have washed their feet before they go to the ceremony.

They will have done it partly out of concern for the one doing the washing – we all know the jokes about smelly feet. They will have done it to protect themselves, too – feet are such personal things; we don't like people messing about with them. Feet are very vulnerable: they get blistered and calloused, corns and bunions make them painful – and anyone getting near our feet might tickle them. We'd be helpless, at their mercy.

We understand all that. And we understand Peter's reluctance to have his feet washed too – not for any of our reasons – Peter, after all, like his friends, would have been used to having his feet washed. It was part of the normal courtesy of hospitality in a hot, dusty country, where guests were refreshed on arrival at their destination with water for footwashing. But this was different. This was Jesus, their leader, taking on a servant's role, doing a woman's work. And Peter's instinctive reaction was to say, 'Surely it should be the other way round, me kneeling before you?' Jesus meets his objection by saying, 'Let me serve you. Let me meet you as you are, and minister to you.'

It's hard to let others minister to us. When Jesus said, 'It is more blessed to give than to receive' (Acts 20.35) he could have added, 'and easier,' too. Most of us are fiercely independent, and we have to learn the willingness to receive graciously. Otherwise, if we are always the ones who give, we diminish others by implying that they are the ones in need, while we are all right. Jesus didn't say, 'Go and wash *everyone else's* feet', he said, 'Wash *one another's* feet' (John 13.14). There has to be a mutuality of service. Jesus modelled that himself, when he let someone wash his feet. Remember the woman, emotional, over the top with her extravagance (Luke 7.37–48)? Scandalous, really, that she should think she had anything to give Jesus, especially in view of her background. But Jesus didn't refuse her ministrations – he knew that she needed to express deep gratitude for her acceptance, and for the forgiveness that had set her free.

So we have to learn to be on the receiving end, as well as doing the washing. Washing people's feet has nothing to do with making them pleasanter to be with. It has everything to do with making people feel welcome, loved and cared for.

And it is hard. People don't turn up on our doorstep with ready-washed feet. They come with dirty feet, feet misshapen by experience, blistered, smelly. And Jesus says that's where we have to get stuck in. It won't always, perhaps even often, be a physical soap and water job. But there will be times when we have the opportunity to minister to someone, to meet them at their point of need; not to make them more acceptable to us, but to help them live with themselves, to begin to understand what it means to be loved.

And if we don't do it? Well, have you noticed that there were two bowls of water called for that night? Jesus took his, filled it with water, and used it to wash feet (John 13.5). Symbol, he said, of love. Pilate sent for his and used it to wash his hands of responsibility (Matthew 27.24).

The bowls are constantly before us. Into which will we dip our hands?

Intercessions for Maundy Thursday

On this night, Lord Jesus, you gave us the command to wash one another's feet. Give us generosity of spirit, so that we may meet each other at the point of need, and accept each other's ministry with grace.
Lord, in your mercy, **hear our prayer.**

On this night, Lord Jesus, you gave us yourself, to be found and remembered in the bread and wine which, blessed by your grace, are our spiritual food and drink. Build us up into your Body, to witness to your love in the world. May we feed on you in our hearts, digest your power; let your life stream through our senses, and energize our thought. May we recall your presence thankfully, a constant savouring.
Lord, in your mercy, **hear our prayer.**

On this night, Lord Jesus, you were betrayed, denied, deserted. Draw us to the foot of your cross, and keep us faithful.
Lord, in your mercy, **hear our prayer.**

On this night, suffering Lord, your heart of love is being torn apart again as aggression and oppression continue in many parts of the world: in . . . . and many places which have slipped from our screens and our memories. Forgive us, Lord. Forgive those who do not know what they are doing, and those who know very well what they do. Draw us to your wounded side, and turn our hearts, and the hearts of all who oppress others, to work for your peace.
Lord, in your mercy, **hear our prayer.**

We pray for all who are trying to meet the needs of others, for all who are trying to establish peace, and we pray that we may play our part, helpless as we often feel.
Lord, those two bowls are before us. Give us wisdom and courage to choose to serve you in one another, and to love as you love us.
Merciful father, accept these prayers, **for the sake of all that your Son accomplished on this night. Amen.**

Eucharistic Prayer for Maundy Thursday

God our Father,
we gather on this night
in praise and gratitude
that you come to us in love,
and that in your Son, Jesus Christ,
you have shown us
how your love must be shared
by honouring and serving others.
With angels and archangels
and all who have tried
to respond to you in humble service,
we worship you, saying:
Holy, holy, holy Lord,
vulnerable God,
heaven and earth are
full of your glory.

Come to us now, Lord God,
as we meet to break bread
and share Christ's life,
who, on the night before he died
took bread and wine, blessed them
and gave them to his friends, saying,
'This is my body, given for you.
This is my blood, shed for you.
Do this to remember me.'

Pour out your Spirit on us now, Lord God,
as we bring before you these gifts
of bread and wine, and remember
Christ's sacrifice made once for all
upon the cross.
Nourish us with his life
that we may live and grow in him.

Give us his spirit of service
that we may love as he loves us.

Take from us all fear that the
cost will be too great:
Keep us faithful, keep us joyful;
for you are the God who delights in us,
and in Christ has called us your friends.

To you, Father, Son and Holy Spirit
be praise and glory, world without end. **Amen.**

Good Friday

These three meditations, lasting one, two and three hours to cater for most requirements, are suitable either for congregational use, or for individuals wanting material to use on their own. They are all based on sections lasting 20 minutes, and are intended to encourage periods of reflection within each section.

In the two- and three-hour services, it is not expected that the Bible passages should be read aloud – they are there for people to use if they find them helpful, so Bibles should be available.

I have found it useful to provide an outline of whichever set of material I have been using, giving times, topics for each section, Bible references and hymn numbers, so that announcements can be kept to a minimum. It is helpful to have this information to give to people who come in part way through the service, to help them orientate themselves.

The guiding principle behind these acts of worship is to leave plenty of time for personal reflection. People very quickly get used to silences lasting between five and ten minutes, even if it is not their normal practice.

The sacred tree – one hour

I

Sing: 'Bless the Lord, my soul' (Taizé)

Bless the Lord, my soul, and bless God's holy name, Bless the Lord, my soul, who leads me into life.

Introduction

American Indians tell the story of a sacred tree, which the Creator has planted. Under it all the people of the earth may gather, and find healing, power, wisdom and security. The roots of this tree spread deep into mother earth, its branches reach up like praying hands to father sky. The fruits of this tree are all the good things the Creator has given to his people: love, compassion, generosity, patience, wisdom, justice, courage, respect, humility, and many other wonderful gifts.

Their ancient teachers taught that the life of the tree is the life of the people. If the people wander far from the tree, if they forget to seek nourishment from its fruit, or if they turn against the tree, and try to destroy it, great sorrow will come to them. Many will become sick at heart, they will cease to dream and see visions, they will begin to quarrel among themselves over worthless things. They will be unable to tell the truth, and deal with each other honestly. They will forget how to survive in their own land. Their lives will become filled with gloom. Little by little, they will poison themselves and all they touch.

But the tree would never die. As long as the tree is alive, the people would live, and one day they would come to their senses, and begin to search for the tree and its truth. Wise elders and leaders have preserved knowledge of the tree, and they will guide anyone who is sincerely seeking for it.

We have come to spend time at the foot of our sacred tree, the cross. There is a medieval poem called *The Dream of the Rood*, which describes the crucifixion from the point of view of the cross, the tree that was cut down and used as a shameful support for a dying man. But the tree says that, much to his surprise, he wasn't the support for a dead weight, but rather the mount for a triumphant Christ, who rode him like a victor in battle. Here is a modern version of the same idea.

Poem: Rood-tree

I might have been his cradle,
Rocking him, folding
Securely against harm.
I could have been a ship,
Turning my sturdy timbers
To the wind, keeping him
Safe from storm.

Instead they used me as
His cross.

No infant rages rocked the
Cradle tree, or storm lashed ship
Such as unleashed on me
That day. Shock waves of hatred
Crashed against me, bearing
On me through his body
Weight of world's pain,
Weight of his agony;
Wringing from him
Drop by drop,
'Why, God, you too?'

No comforting protection
Could I offer, or deliverance;
Only support, his mainstay in distress.

But did I hold him, or did he
With strength of purpose lovingly

Embrace his work of suffering,
Stretched on my arms?

They say it was a tree whose fruit
Brought sorrow to the world.
The fruit I bore,
Though seeming shame,
They call salvation.

My glory was it then,
To be his tree.[1]

The cross is not ashamed to be associated with Christ, and nor should we, marked with the sign of the cross, be ashamed to bear him with us in our world.

Silence, ending with the prayer:

May we, signed with the sign of the cross, never be ashamed to confess the faith of Christ crucified, for the sake of him who died and lives for the world, Jesus Christ. **Amen.**

Hymn: 'When I survey the wondrous cross'

II

In the old Genesis story, it was the fruit of a tree which brought our downfall. Was that an apple tree? But there were two trees mentioned in that story, and God didn't forbid the fruit of both of them.

Poem: Two trees (Genesis 2.9)

God did not say
'You must not eat
Fruit of the Tree of Life.'
But burdened by guilt
At tasting the forbidden fruit
Of the other tree, our energy

Is spent in dealing with our
Dreadful knowledge of
Good and evil.

And all the while,
The Tree of Life offers us
Nourishment.

Eat its fruit, and live.[2]

When Adam and Eve left the Garden, the way to the tree of life was guarded, so that they couldn't get back to it. But between that time and this Christ has opened the way to life, and he invites us to feed on the life that he gives.

Another medieval poem, 'Jesus Christ the apple tree', talks about Jesus as a tree.

Think of all the things trees provide: protection and shelter, warmth, a meeting place, nourishment, healing. Jesus is all these things.

Sing or listen to: Elizabeth Poston's setting of 'Jesus Christ the apple tree'.

Jesus offers us new life, so in the silence now, we ponder on this gift.

Fragment

Feed on him in your hearts, digest his power;
Let his life slow release itself into your blood,
Stream through your senses, energize your thoughts.
Recall his presence thankfully,
A constant savouring.[3]

Silence, ending with the prayer:

Father, we give you thanks that the tree of shame was made the tree of glory, and that where life was lost, there life has been restored, in Jesus Christ our Lord. **Amen.**

III

And what of us?

The Letter to the Ephesians offers us tree pictures too.

Reading: Ephesians 3.14–19

The imagery of the tree is strong: we in our turn are to be trees, nourishing the hidden life of our roots through prayer, Bible reading, worship; and letting the visible part of our life offer to the world all that Christ the tree offers us.

Poem: Christ the tree

Deep-rooted in the
Love of God the Father,
Moving, responding to
The Spirit's power;
Drawing all people
By your ageless
Wisdom, giving
To all who come
Healing and strength;
Life bursting forth,
Disturbing, powerful;
Cut down,
But bearing fruit.

Here I will rest,
And wait until sap rises,
Your life in mine,
My resurrection.[4]

Our roots need to go deep. Roots are powerful, and what roots us in the love of God is prayer.

Poem: Prayer tree

Prayer gives us rootedness,
Reaching out,
Discovering in darkness
Sources of nourishment;
Pushing with patient insistence
Against obstacles;
Drawing from strange places
Strength for life that
Grows in light;
Holding us as we bend,
And when we break, offering
Hope, that from the
Unimaginable dark,
New shoots will spring.[5]

We need to stay close to Christ the tree, but the nourishment Christ gives has to bear fruit: it is not just for our benefit, but for the sake of the world.

Silence, ending with the prayer:

Lord God, nourish us so that we bear fruit for you and offer healing and peace to all around, for the sake of your Son, who was lifted up so that the world might be saved.

Hymn: 'There in God's garden stands the tree of wisdom'

Blessing

Notes

1. *Watching for the Kingfisher*, p. 86.
2. Ibid., p. 22.
3. Ibid., p. 63.
4. Ibid., p. 22.
5. Ibid., p. 23.

Seen by the cross – two hours

Hymn: 'We sing the praise of him who died'

'Seen by the cross' is a title which can be taken two ways. There were people close to the cross as Jesus was crucified – Mary his mother, the beloved disciple, the soldiers and the centurion. A little further off, perhaps wanting to get closer, but not allowed any nearer, the women, among them Mary Magdalene, and Peter, unless he was so heartbroken at the way things had turned out that he couldn't bear to be there. And the cross itself, if it could speak, would have noted their presence. Perhaps it would also have noted the absence of two people who had been prominent in the run-up to the crucifixion, but who had chosen to go a different way.

Judas and Pilate may seem a strange pair to link together, for their allegiance lay in different directions. But both of them were driven by their own agenda, which in the end proved to be too strong to allow them to stay with Jesus.

Judas

Judas is thought to have been a Zealot, a member of a political party aiming at the overthrow of the Roman government. He couldn't wait for Jesus to get on with it. A few days before, it had seemed as though the moment had come: there was Jesus, entering Jerusalem in triumph – it could have happened then. Of course, it would have been better if Jesus had ridden into the city on a horse, like a real conqueror, instead of looking a bit stupid on a donkey. But the people were with him: 'Hosanna, save us now,' they had yelled. And then what happened? Endless talk, upsetting people in the Temple. He'd miss his chance if he wasn't careful. Worse, the way he was going on, he'd get himself killed for the wrong reason. Perhaps if he was put in a position where he'd have to fight or die, he would get on with it. So the plans were laid. The religious leaders didn't care what Judas' motives were, so long as he told them where they could find Jesus away from the crowds. A small reward – he could have held out for a big one, but it wasn't the money, it was the Cause that mattered.

And then the awful realization that he'd got it wrong. His attempts to rescue the situation failed. And he felt that his life was not worth living (Matthew 26.14–16, 47–49, 27.3–10).

Pilate

Pilate was in a different position. He was running scared. It had been a difficult job from the beginning. Whatever pleasure he might have had from his promotion to governorship was spoilt by fear that he might not be man enough for the job. He'd decided right at the start that he would show the Jews who was boss. He marched into Jerusalem to take up his post, with the Roman eagle carried proudly at the head of the cavalcade. Redecoration of his new home included some of the same emblems. The Jews threatened to report him to his superiors for provoking them by bringing emblems of a foreign god into their holy city. When he showed no signs of giving in, they demonstrated outside his palace. He was no match for a chanting mob, and the decorations were removed.

He'd trodden warily ever since, and mostly the province had been quiet and peaceful. But now there was another threat, the Jesus business. Pilate couldn't understand what the fuss was about – the fellow seemed harmless enough, even positively good. Pilate had heard about his care for people and his healing power. There didn't seem to be any hint of his rebelling against Caesar – in fact, when he'd been challenged Jesus had quite clearly said that people ought to give Caesar his due.

So when the Jewish leaders came and asked him to get rid of Jesus, his first instinct was to have nothing to do with it.

He tried very hard to avoid sending Jesus to his death – but when he heard the words 'If you let this man go you are not Caesar's friend', his blood ran cold. 'Not Caesar's friend' meant he was Caesar's enemy, and that spelt death for him. So he called for a bowl of water, and washed his hands of the whole affair (Matthew 27.11–26).

But someone else had taken a bowl of water earlier that night, and washed his disciples' feet, a symbol of the loving service he wanted his followers to engage in (John 13.1–20). Those two bowls represent the choice always before us. Will we follow Christ's example, throw in our lot with him? Or will we let a different agenda run our lives? The bowls are always before us. Into which will we dip our hands?

Silence

Prayer

Lord God,
draw us ever closer to you.
When we are faced with difficult choices,
help us to seek your will;
when we are frightened
for our personal safety,
give us courage;
when we are challenged with others' need,
give us compassion;
for the sake of Jesus Christ our Lord. **Amen.**

1.20 p.m. Hymn: 'O word of pity for our pardon pleading'

Peter

Perhaps we identify more easily with Peter than we do with Judas and Pilate. After all, he didn't make a choice to force Jesus' hand, or wash his hands of any responsibility for what happened to Jesus. He was caught out by weakness, rather than making a deliberate choice. Perhaps that's what happens to us too.

Peter had always been an enthusiastic follower, even if he hadn't always got things right. He sometimes blurted words out without thinking first – sometimes he got it gloriously right, like the time he said that Jesus was the Christ, the Messiah. And sometimes he got it horribly wrong – almost immediately after that great confession of faith, he got a stinging rebuke from Jesus when he said that the Messiah didn't need to suffer as Jesus said he would. But he'd learnt that Jesus didn't hold it against people when they got things wrong, if they were genuinely trying. Jesus hadn't said, 'You're not the rock I thought you were.' He'd gone on putting his faith in Peter, taking him with James and John on some significant occasions, like the Transfiguration, and into the Garden of Gethsemane; calming things down when Peter's enthusiasm got a bit out of hand, as it did when he attacked one of the soldiers in the Garden.

But what happened after the arrest had brought Peter to despair. Jesus had warned them that they would be put to a severe test that night. And Peter had been so sure that he wouldn't let Jesus down – 'Even if the rest deny you, I won't,' he'd said. And Jesus had said that before cock-crow, Peter would have denied him three times.

We know what happened. Peter followed at a distance when Jesus was led off, and in those long dark hours three times he was approached in the courtyard, and three times he denied being anything to do with Jesus.

At the point when Jesus was led out to be crucified, through the courtyard where Peter was trying to keep warm by the fire, the cock crowed. Luke tells us that Jesus turned and looked at Peter – and Peter remembered how Jesus had warned him that this would happen. And he went out and wept bitterly (Luke 22.24–34, 54–62).

That response of Peter's tells us something about Jesus' look. If it had been the kind of look that says, 'I told you so', Peter's response would probably have been to get defensive

– 'What did you expect? I didn't think you'd go to those lengths. I've got a wife and family to support – I couldn't put my life on the line.' But that wasn't his response. He wept bitterly. The look must surely have been a look of love, that said, 'I know you, Peter – and you are still the rock on which I will build.' Such love and understanding would move anyone to tears.

So, would Peter have been there at the cross? I think he would. I think he had begun to get a glimmer of the truth that Jesus reinforced for him after the resurrection: that nothing we do can stop God loving us. And we can be there too, longing to love, not always getting things right, but beginning to realize the love of God which nothing can destroy.

Silence

Prayer

In our sight we do not stand,
in God's sight we do not fall.
Both these insights are true,
but the greater belongs to God.
Merciful God, help us to grasp this truth,
and hold it fast, for the sake of your Son,
Jesus Christ. **Amen.**

Based on words from Julian of Norwich

1.40 p.m. Hymn: 'Just as I am, without one plea'

Mary

Standing by the cross was his mother. How do we identify with her?

Medieval devotion and catholic piety have conspired to put her on a pedestal – an unattainable figure of virtue who isn't like us at all.

You always appear too good to be true, Mary.
We've pictured you always serene,
Never exasperated by a fractious child,
Apparently having no feelings.

But surely that initial Yes came
From a moment of overwhelming terror,
And the birth tore you to the core?
Didn't he ever cry, that baby,
Give you sleepless nights?
Didn't he irritate you,
That precocious son
Dismissing your anxiety with
Didn't you know? And later
That wounding question
Who is my mother?
My mother would have told him . . .
Perhaps you did too,
But it wasn't recorded.[1]

There are many indications in the Gospels that Mary was baffled by her son. Pondering on the events surrounding his birth may have been a source of comfort to her – but may have increased her bewilderment too. Jesus had been ordinary enough as a boy, learning the values of God's kingdom at Mary's knee and Joseph's bench. There was that puzzling event in the Temple when he was 12, when he seemed to be laying claim to another source of authority (Luke 2.41–51). But they had weathered that as a family, and Jesus had remained at home with them until the moment came for him to begin his public work. Then it seemed that he was abandoning his family to establish another set of relationships with all those who were intent on doing God's will. 'Who is my mother, and who are my brothers? . . . For whoever does the will of my Father in heaven is my brother and sister and mother' (Matthew 12.49–50). Perhaps Mary remembered then the words of Simeon when her baby was six weeks old:

'This child is destined for the falling and rising of many in Israel, and to be a sign that will be opposed so that the inner thoughts of many will be revealed – and a sword will pierce your own soul too' (Luke 2.34–35).

I don't think that sword waited until the crucifixion to pierce her heart – there were other moments when it must have felt that a knife was twisting within her.

Mary and the rest of the family seem to have followed Jesus' activities, even if they weren't part of the inner circle of his followers. It must have been very hard for Mary to see her son running into opposition, apparently asking for trouble. Bittersweet the realization that all his words and actions echoed her Magnificat, as he taught and preached the kingdom values she must have taught him.

And then the hardest thing of all, to be there watching him die, not even being able to touch him to bring him comfort. Surely that wouldn't have been a Mary serene in her grief as artists portray her. Much more like those ravaged faces we see on our screens, raging at the senseless killing of the innocent.

It's in our rage and pain that we can stand at the cross, too, and begin to feel the saving power of one who comes to us with wounded hands, to cradle us in love.

Silence

Prayer

Lord, with wounded hands we pray that you will cradle your world in your love. Heal your suffering people, and restore your exploited creation, that we may all learn to honour one another, and live in wholeness to your glory. **Amen.**

2.00 p.m. Hymn: 'O sacred head'

The beloved disciple

'Jesus saw his mother, and the disciple whom he loved standing beside her' (John 19.26–27).

The beloved disciple appears only in John's Gospel – at least, he's only described in that way by John. We don't know who he is, but he is clearly very close to Jesus.

He appears first at the account of the Last Supper, where he is described as lying close to the breast of Jesus (John 13.23–25). Peter asked him to find out who Jesus had been talking about as the betrayer. The beloved disciple, in the intimacy of that closeness, asked, 'Lord, who is it?'

We see him at the cross, and then again at the resurrection, when in response to Mary Magdalene bringing the news that the Lord's body is not in the tomb, he runs with Peter, reaches the tomb first but does not go in, leaving Peter to do that. But it is the beloved disciple who saw and believed (John 20.1–8).

He is also the subject of Peter's question, after Peter's restoration when he is called again to follow Jesus. Peter sees the beloved disciple and asks, 'What about him?' And Jesus says in effect, 'That's a matter for him and me. You take responsibility for your own calling' (John 21.20–23).

So we really don't know much about him, except that he was very close to Jesus, close enough at times to hear his heart beat. And he stayed close, right up to the cross, entering into the pain and suffering of his Lord. Because he was there, he was entrusted with the care of Jesus' mother, and because he had been close, he understood, in a way that Peter didn't at first, what the victory of the cross over sin and death was. He saw beneath the surface, and believed.

So who was he? It doesn't matter. He was the beloved disciple, one whom Jesus loved. He was each one of us, loved as we are. He gives us the clue to discipleship: that it begins and is undergirded by staying very close to Jesus; that it will take us to the heart of suffering; that it gives us a responsibility for others, and that it gives us insights into the nature of eternal life, that quality of life that transcends death and keeps us close to the heartbeat of God.

Silence

Prayer

God, of your goodness, give us yourself, for if we ask anything that is less than can do you full worship, we shall always be in want. Only in you we have all. **Amen.**

From Julian of Norwich

2.20 p.m. Hymn: 'My God, I love thee'

Mary Magdalene

Who was she? There's confusion about her identity, because several stories in the Gospels could be about her. There's a story Luke tells (Luke 7.36–50) of a woman who was a sinner who burst into tears over Jesus, anointed him with precious ointment and dried his feet with her hair. Jesus recognized her penitence, her desire to change. He drew attention to the fact that a realization of forgiveness brings a response of love, and sends her on her way a new woman. John told of a similar event (John 12.1–8) and identified the woman with Mary of Bethany. So she had a name.

Luke also tells us about the women who supported Jesus, among them Mary Magdalene from whom seven devils were cast out (Luke 8.1–3). There has been much speculation about those devils: in the history of the Christian Church, the area of human life about which people seem to have had the most hang-ups is sexual desire and relationships. So it was a very short step to say that her problem lay in her sexual behaviour – she must have been a prostitute. It is more likely that people possessed with demons were suffering from what we have learned to call mental illness – they were ill, not evil.

Artists have often portrayed Mary Magdalene weeping, and that gave rise to our word maudlin – weak, sentimental, tearful – like some people are when they've had too much to drink. And there was a kind of social work called Magdalen care up to the mid-nineteenth century, primarily providing for women and girls in moral danger, some of whom were prostitutes.

So mention of Mary Magdalene would cause people to give each other a nudge and a wink, and say she was no better than she should be. But when we look at the evidence in the Gospels, all that we can say is that she came from Magdala, a commercial town with a big fishing fleet on the shores of Lake Gennesaret; she was healed by Jesus – whatever the seven devils represented was put to rights, and her response was to support Jesus with her friendship. She became the leader of a group of women who contributed from their wealth to keep the Jesus movement on its feet. Far from being maudlin, she was strong, someone with leadership qualities, who stayed faithful right to the end; there at the cross, going to the burial place to do what was necessary to ensure that her Lord had a proper burial (John 19.25, 20.1–8). Perhaps it doesn't matter who she was – she was like all of us, a mixture:

> Damaged and healed,
> Longing to be loved
> And struggling to relate;
> Passionate and reserved
> By turns, working out
> Costly discipleship.[2]

The important moment for her was when she was called by name. And that's our important moment, too, when with all our confusions and questions about our identity, we realize that we are known by name and loved by God. And as Mary was sent out to spread the good news, so are we. For being known and loved by God doesn't bring us into a cosy relationship, it is the basis of our witness to the love of God for everyone.

Silence

Prayer

My God, I desire to love thee
with all my heart
which thou madest for thyself;
with all my mind
which only thou canst satisfy;
with all my soul,
which longs to soar to thee;
with all my strength, my feeble strength,
which shrinks before so great a task,
and yet can choose nought else
but spend itself in loving thee.

Claim thou my heart,
fill thou my mind,
uplift my soul and
reinforce my strength,
that where I fail,
thou mayest succeed in me,
and make me love thee perfectly.

W. H. Frere

2.40 p.m. Hymn: 'My God accept my heart this day'

The cross

If the cross could speak, what story would it tell? Right at the centre of the picture, was it an instrument of shame and degradation, or a place of victory?

Depictions of the cross in art and literature have followed the insights of theology. In early centuries, artists rarely focused on the suffering of Christ, rather on his victory. The earliest known depiction of the crucifixion, from Rome in about 420, shows Christ standing upright on the cross, his eyes open, his body unmarked by suffering, a victor over death. It was not until some centuries later, when theology moved the emphasis from the work of God the Father to the suffering of God the Son, that the man of sorrows became the model for the figure on the cross.

There is an Anglo-Saxon poem that expresses a strong belief that the cross was about glory. Called *The Dream of the Rood*, the poem describes how the dreamer heard the cross describe what the experience of bearing the crucified Christ was like. In it the cross speaks of the way it was set in place, prepared to bear the weight of the one being crucified, only to find that he came to the cross not as an abject victim, but as a warrior, mounting the cross and fighting for the salvation of humankind. Undoubtedly, crucifixion was a shameful death in the eyes of Jews and Romans alike. But to the eye of faith, the tree of shame became the tree of glory, and where life was lost, there life has been restored.

We are called not just to stand at the cross, but to take up our cross – to witness to the victory won on that Good Friday. We trivialize the idea of taking up the cross when we use the phrase to describe putting up with things we don't like. 'It's the cross I have to bear,' we say, in the tone of voice that is meant to evoke sympathy for our plight. But that is self-indulgence. Taking up the cross has a sharper edge to it – and we don't have to manufacture our cross. Perhaps we would be closer to the truth if we were to think of it as being true to the cross with which we were signed at baptism. Taking up our cross means being true to that sign, bearing Christ with us wherever we go. Bearing witness to our belief that God really has overcome the evil in the world – always looking for God in the intractable areas of suffering and exploitation and grief, as well as rejoicing in God's presence where we experience life. Taking up our cross will mean challenging the forces that exploit or destroy, affirming the people who build up and encourage. It's not a path that will bring us instant popularity or success – for Jesus it meant crucifixion. But as Julian of Norwich said, 'He did not say you will not be tested, he said you will not be overcome.'

Silence

Prayer

We adore you, O Christ, and we bless you, because by your cross you have redeemed the world. **Amen.**

Hymn: 'When I survey the wondrous cross'

2.55 p.m. Conclusion

We stand at the foot of the cross, where this great work of salvation has been unfolding.

The last word is with the centurion, who had watched all this going on too, and found himself at something of a crossroads (Mark 15.39).

Poem: Crossroads

I cursed my luck, on duty in that heat:
The flies, the blood, the stench of death.
It was the loneliest place I've ever known,
Standing beside that cross. The crowds,
Hurling abuse, engulfed me with their hate;
Had he no friends? Standing not far away,
The women had more courage than the men,
But even his God, it seemed, had left him.
I've seen some crucifixions in my time,
But never one like this: the victim

More concerned for others than himself,
Asking forgiveness for his murderers.
And then that aweful darkness, when
The world died with him, and the cry that
Pierced the darkness pierced me too.
Did he say, 'Finished'? The way I feel
It's only just begun.[3]

Dismissal

And now we go out to continue the story.

In the name of Christ. Amen.

Notes

1. From 'Get real', in *Watching for the Kingfisher*, p. 34.
2. From 'Known by Name', in *Watching for the Kingfisher*, p. 70.
3. *Watching for the Kingfisher*, p. 87.

Seen by the cross – three extra sections

(Three extra sections which could be used in the middle hour to extend the 'Seen by the cross – two hours' to a three-hour meditation)

Simon of Cyrene

We don't often think of Simon being in the crowd at the Crucifixion. He's one of the bit-part actors on the way – it could have been anyone who was ordered to help carry Jesus' cross. But it was a man who is named, and identified as a foreigner, an African. Was he someone who happened to be in the wrong place, caught up in the ignominy of a criminal's journey to crucifixion? Or was he there because he knew Jesus? Had he been following him, listening to his teaching? Had he perhaps already committed himself to the Jesus way? Perhaps this really was the moment that changed his life, just as the direction of his journey was turned round, for he was going towards Jerusalem before he was made to go in the other direction with Jesus. We don't know. But we do know that he, and his sons Alexander and Rufus, were well enough known in the Christian community by the time that Mark wrote his Gospel, for him to be identified as the one who was pressed into service. So if he hadn't been convinced by Jesus' life, he was convinced by the manner of his dying, and the new life that followed from that event. And his sons came too.

It wasn't what he'd planned – if he was there intentionally, it would probably have been, like the others, to follow at a distance. But he found himself, foreigner that he was, right in the middle of the action. And if Jesus had been in a position to do so, he might well have flung his arms round him in gratitude. But the only place where he could open his arms wide was on the cross – for the foreigner as well as everyone else.

What about us? Do we welcome foreigners and strangers? Overseas visitors perhaps, but asylum seekers? What do we make of Government policies about them? We've been involved in combating the injustice of poverty in the developing world. Are we equally committed to ensuring that people who come to this country seeking a new life are treated with justice and compassion? Perhaps we don't meet many of them where we live – but it is in our name that policies are made. Do we make our views known? Do we welcome seasonal workers? Do we know how they are treated? Do we care?

We are Christ's body now – he has no other on earth. Ours are the eyes with which he is to look with compassion on the world; ours the feet on which he is to go about doing good; ours the voice with which kind, encouraging and challenging words are to be spoken; ours the hands with which Christ will bless people now. The gospel truth is that Jesus opened his arms wide for everyone, on the Cross. As Christ's body do we open our arms wide to care for people too? Or do we tie Christ's hands again?

Silence

Prayer

Lord Jesus Christ, you stretched out your arms of love on the hard wood of the cross, that everyone might come within the reach of your saving embrace: so clothe us in your Spirit that we, reaching forth our hands in love, may bring those who do not know you to knowledge and love of you, for the honour of your name. **Amen.**

Bishop Charles Henry Brent 1862–1929

Hymn: 'Brother, sister, let me serve you'

The soldiers and bystanders

The soldiers had a job to do. They were hardened to cruelty and suffering – if you were carrying out a crucifixion you couldn't afford to get sentimental. Perhaps the only way you could cope was to mock and jeer, and try to get some reaction from the victim which would make you feel your actions were justified. One or two of them, it seemed, did make a gesture, offering a drink to a dying man, but on the whole, if not hostile they were indifferent. Once they'd got the victims on their crosses, all they could do was wait for them to die – and while away the time by dividing their clothes up among themselves – pretty inadequate perks for the job. Cruel, hostile, indifferent, they were doing their job.

But the soldiers weren't the only ones there. There were some bystanders too. The inevitable lookers-on when there is something dramatic going on. What about them? Some of them, identified as their leaders, joined in the mockery. None, it seemed, did anything to make life easier for the victims. Sometimes the sins of *permission* are as harmful as the sins we more readily recognize, of *commission* and *omission.* Standing by and not getting actively involved doesn't mean that we have no part in what is going on, we are all involved simply by being fellow human beings.

How do we respond to all the evil and cruelty around us? Jesus told us to pray for our enemies, for people who abuse and hurt us. It's easy to pray for people we feel concern for, the victims of crime or abuse, or people we know who are going through a hard time. But the others? Can we pray for those who carry out the abuse, perpetrate the evil? Part of our difficulty perhaps lies in the feeling that when we pray for someone, we are concerned for their wellbeing, and that might seem like showing approval for what they do. But the wellbeing of those who perpetrate evil would come about through God's light and love penetrating their hearts and minds, and bringing them to realize that there is a better way, God's way. Not just *their* hearts and minds, *ours* too. For we are not the good people who are in a position of superiority, praying for the baddies who don't behave in an acceptable way. The fault line runs through each one of us. Only those who have never had an unkind thought about their neighbours, or have never stood by without protest as something bad was happening, could ever claim to be superior. Not many of us could lay claim to that state. 'Lord have mercy' is a prayer we all need to pray, for ourselves as well as others.

Silence

Prayer

Lord Jesus, as you opened your arms wide on the cross, you prayed for those who were crucifying you, 'Father forgive them, for they know not what they do.' Forgive us, who usually know very well what we do, and penetrate the darkness in all of us with your light and love. Bring us all to a desire to honour one another, and seek the common good.

Hymn: 'For the healing of the nations'

The two thieves

There were two thieves crucified with Jesus. They had definite reactions to Christ. They had heard all the taunts being thrown at him – he saved others, but he can't save himself – what price now being the chosen one, the Christ, it doesn't seem to amount to much.

One of the thieves joined in, not mocking, in real anger and pain. 'If you are the Christ, save yourself and us.' But the other one rebuked him: 'We are being punished for what we have done. But this man has done nothing wrong.' Then he turned to Jesus, with what was really a confession of faith: 'Lord, remember me when you come into your kingdom.'

And Jesus responded with his arms opened wide: 'Today you will be with me in paradise.'

There are two ways to respond to realizing that we have done something wrong. One is to deny responsibility, and try to push the blame or attention onto someone else: if I'd been treated differently, if you had behaved differently, I wouldn't have done what I did. The other is to accept responsibility and ask for forgiveness: 'Lord, remember me.'

By his response to the one we call the penitent thief, Jesus indicates that the latter is the way to the Kingdom. Penitence does not consist in using extravagant language about how sinful we are, or in carrying inappropriate guilt, or allowing feelings of worthlessness to colour our lives. Mother Julian of Norwich (fourteenth century) said that all those are much more damaging than the sin which we have to acknowledge in the first place. If we feel that we have cut ourselves off from God by our sin, it is a barrier that is built from our side, not God's. For nothing can stop God loving us. That is not to say that sin doesn't matter. 'It is the worst scourge with which the soul can be struck,' she said. But God's love is unwavering. God looks at us 'with compassion, not with blame. In our sight we do not stand, in God's sight we do not fall. Both these insights are true, but the greater belongs to God'. And it's that greater insight on which we should focus our attention. Penitence should never leave us looking at ourselves, but looking at Christ, through whom we receive forgiveness. Our prayer, 'Lord have mercy', as we acknowledge our responsibility for our sin, brings the ready response from God in Christ on the cross. Jesus opens his arms wide for us, as he did for the two thieves: there is nothing that will get in the way of our being enfolded in his embrace today, if only we will acknowledge our need of his forgiving love.

Silence

Prayer

Lord, you are the God who forgives and heals.
Come to us now, move our hearts
To deeper repentance, and enfold us
In your loving embrace. May your forgiveness
Set us free to love and serve you
with the whole of our being.

Hymn: 'Lord Jesus, think on me'

Prayer at the cross – three hours

In this three hours, we shall follow Jesus through the week leading up to the crucifixion, and look at prayer in the light of his experience. After the introduction, in each 20-minute section, there will be a period of silence for reflection and prayer. The words from a Psalm or one of the Prophets, printed in the order of service, may help you to focus on the theme. Each period of silence will end with a poem or a prayer, and a hymn.

We begin where Jesus began, as we sing the hymn: 'Ride on, ride on in majesty'.

Prayer as encounter

Jesus rides into Jerusalem: Mark 11.1–11.

On Palm Sunday, Jesus rode into his city, and the people knew exactly what he had come for. 'Save us now,' they shouted, 'Hosanna to the Son of David!'

But they misread the signs. Jesus was riding a donkey, not a horse; he'd come in humility, not earthly power. And he didn't do what people expected. He didn't start a revolt, he went to the Temple and looked around.

We come to prayer, often, thinking we know what it's about. We lay before God our hopes, our fears, our demands and requirements; we say, 'Your will be done', and often mean 'Lord, do it my way.' But prayer is always a searching experience. We read in 1 Corinthians 3.16, 'Do you not know that you are God's temple, and that God's Spirit dwells in you?' Prayer is an engagement on God's terms, not ours; we come in response to his call, not to do him a favour. And when we draw near in prayer, he will look around us, his temples.

Metropolitan Anthony Bloom reminded us that this God with whom we have to do is not a tame cat, but a tiger. Before

God, all we can do is stand, or kneel, or fall on our faces in awe and wonder.[1]

To ponder in the stillness

O come, let us worship and bow down,
Let us kneel before the LORD, our Maker!
For he is our God.

Psalm 95.6–7

Silence

Prayer

Lord God, you reveal yourself in simple ways, yet you are greater by far than our imagining. We praise you for your great glory. **Amen.**

12.20 p.m. Hymn: 'My God, how wonderful thou art'

The prayer of anger

The cleansing of the Temple: Mark 11.15–17.

Palm Sunday over, there were mixed feelings about what Jesus had come to do. The next day, Jesus came back to the Temple and drove out the money-changers, and those buying and selling animals for sacrifice, with some violence. You remember the layout of the Temple: a central Holy of Holies, which only the High Priest could enter, and then only once a year; the Holy Place, where the priests carried out some of their duties; the Court of the Israelites, for the men; the Court of Women, and outside, and beyond all that, the Court of the Gentiles. A place where you had your place, and knew your place. There were rules about what had to happen. Ordinary coins had on them the image of the Emperor, and had to be changed into Temple money with all the dissatisfaction that we experience with exchange rates. Animals for sacrifice had to be without blemish, and the easiest way to ensure that was to acquire them on the spot. All that went on in the court of the Gentiles. There was no peace for prayer there, and the Gentiles could go no further on pain of death. However we try to soften it, the description of this event shows Jesus angry – angry at the way the 'in' crowd excluded the outsiders. 'Is it not written, "My house shall be called a house of prayer for all nations"?' By siting the money-changing and the sales in the court of the Gentiles, the only part of the Temple non-Jews could go into, all non-Jews were prevented from joining in the prayer without noisy distractions.

We don't like to think of Jesus being angry – we find him easier to deal with if he is gentle, meek and mild. Perhaps part of our difficulty with an angry Jesus is that we don't know how to deal with our own anger. We are perhaps frightened by the violence we know within ourselves – perhaps we have been taught from an early age that anger is sinful. And so, often, it is. But at times, anger is God's spur to right wrongs, relieve oppression, see justice done.

If we have begun our prayer by attending to God and worshipping him in his greatness, we have to learn to continue it by looking at the world through his eyes, and recognizing that part of our prayer has to be action which will, as Amos put it, enable 'justice [to] roll down like waters, and righteousness like an ever-flowing stream' (Amos 5.24).

To ponder in the stillness

What does the Lord require of you but to do justice, and to love kindness, and to walk humbly with your God?

Micah 6.8

Silence

Poem: Temple cleansing

Sometimes the only right response is
Anger. Not dull resentment,
Poisoning all it touches, or
Bitterness that taints the memory,
But a clean cutting edge, that
Lances festering grievances,
Releasing energy to fight;
The fuel of passion that
Challenges evils
Outwardly observed
Or known within.
Such anger is not sin.[2]

12.40 p.m. Hymn: 'What does the Lord require for praise and offering', or 'The kingdom of God is justice and joy'

Wrestling with hard questions

Jesus in the Temple: Mark 11.27–33; 12.13–34; 41–44.

Jesus went back to Bethany each night in the early part of the week, but the third day in Holy Week saw Jesus back in the Temple, wrestling with questions about authority, life and death, loyalty to God. One after another the questions came.

First, from the Pharisees – by whose authority? If you can discredit someone, you don't have to listen. And then a couple of trick questions.

Taxation – is it lawful? 'Bring me a coin.' That would have involved a trip back to the money-changers. Jesus wasn't going to be caught out by having a coin in his possession. Whose image is on it? Then give him his due. But give God what is his too.

Then the Sadducees, who didn't believe in life after death, came up with an old chestnut, the one about the woman who married seven brothers in turn. In the resurrection, whose wife would she be?

Each time, Jesus turned the question back, with 'What do you think?' He always does that, he's not one for giving easy answers. Work it out for yourselves, he says. If you've got ears, hear. If you've got minds, think.

We sometimes treat prayer as though it's a magic formula: apply it in the right way, pray properly, and we'll get the answers. But it's not quite like that. Jesus isn't the answer, he's the question, probing our hearts and minds: what do you really think about life and its purpose, how much do you really want to give yourself to God?

Amidst all the questioning, perhaps it's one of the other people Jesus saw that day who gives us the clue, the widow who gave all that she had. Learning what is God's will is rooted in attending to God. The answers to our hard questions emerge from the kind of commitment that the widow had.

To ponder in the stillness

For God alone my soul waits in silence.

Psalm 62.1

Silence

Prayer

Lord Jesus Christ, alive and at large in the world,
Help me to follow and find you there today,
In the places where I work, meet people,
Spend money and make plans.
Take me as a disciple of your kingdom, to see through your eyes,

To hear the questions you are asking,
To welcome all others with your trust and truth,
And to change the things that contradict God's love
By the power of the cross, and the freedom of your
Spirit.

John V. Taylor, from *A Matter of Life and Death*

1.00 p.m. Hymn: 'Be thou my vision'

Prayer as resting

Jesus with his friends: Mark 14.3–9.

On 'Wednesday', Jesus appears to have spent time with his friends in Bethany, and allowed himself to be cared for, made a fuss of by the woman who anointed him. Perhaps we are a bit embarrassed that Jesus lets himself be ministered to. Perhaps we're not very good at letting others minister to us. 'Oh, you shouldn't have,' we say. 'You shouldn't have spent that much on me . . .' One of the disciples said that. 'Fancy spending that much on him.' And these were his friends! We're not very good at accepting. We're not very good at resting either. There's something in our British character that makes us feel we've always got to be on the go. Kipling's version of the Protestant work ethic, in his poem 'If', says it for us:

> If you can fill the unforgiving minute
> With sixty seconds' worth of distance run,
> Yours is the world and everything that's in it

(we won't dwell on the last line, about 'being a man, my son'!).

Yours is the world . . . Jesus said, 'For what will it profit them if they gain the whole world but forfeit their life?' (Matthew 16.26). The Bible is full of invitations to come apart and rest, be still, and know God.

To ponder in the stillness

In returning and rest you shall be saved; in quietness and trust shall be your strength.

Isaiah 30.15

Silence

There's a hymn which begins, 'Father, hear the prayer we offer, not for ease that prayer shall be.' One response to that could be the poem:

Poem: The prayer we offer

Not for ease? Why not?
What's wrong with ease?
For most of us the
Problem is not self-indulgence,
But that we allow ourselves too little.
Prohibitions, counsels of perfection
Drive us and load us up with guilt.

Time enough for courageous living
And all that rock-smiting.
Let's rest and wander in green pastures
When we find them, make the space
To let ourselves be loved;
Build up our strength
And grow in confidence;
Drink living water springing in
Great fountains;
Feed on the Bread of Life which
Satisfies.
Then we shall have provision
For the journey, and at last
Arrive, not too unpractised
In the art of resting
In his presence.[3]

1.20 p.m. Hymn: 'Dear Lord and Father of mankind'

Sharing in God's life

The Last Supper: John 13.1–9; Mark 14.22–24.

Maundy Thursday, New Commandment day.

We find it hard to let others care for us. We find it harder to rest with God. One reason for this is that we don't really believe that God loves us. We can't allow ourselves to think we are lovable.

At the beginning of the passage from John, Jesus washed the disciples' feet. Picture the scene: reclining at the table, perhaps they don't at first realize what Jesus is doing. And then it dawns on them. Our feet are very personal things – they carry the marks of our life in very particular ways, and we don't like people playing with them. The thought of someone else washing our feet, let alone our Lord, is almost too much – and anyway, they might tickle.

So, like Peter, we back off –

What, let you wash my feet?
Shouldn't it be the other way,
Me kneeling before you?[4]

The feeling that we'd be at Christ's mercy if we let him get that close makes us keep him at arm's length, at least.

But first the footwashing, and then the gift of Christ's life as he gives his body and blood, are invitations to us to open ourselves to the love of God, let him love us into wholeness, let him re-form his likeness in us, who were made in his image. We are very special to God.

To ponder in the stillness

. . . you are precious in my sight, and honoured,
and I love you.

Isaiah 43.4

Silence

Poem: Love

Love bade me welcome; yet my soul drew back,
Guilty of dust and sin.
But quick-eyed Love, observing me grow slack
From my first entrance in,
Drew nearer to me, sweetly questioning
If I lacked anything.

'A guest,' I answered, 'worthy to be here':
Love said, 'You shall be he.'
'I, the unkind, ungrateful? Ah, my dear,
I cannot look on Thee.'
Love took my hand, and smiling did reply,
'Who made the eyes but I?'

'Truth, Lord; but I have marr'd them; let my shame
Go where it doth deserve.'
'And know you not,' says Love, 'Who bore the blame?'
'My dear, then I will serve.'
'You must sit down,' says Love, 'and taste My meat.'
So I did sit and eat.

George Herbert

1.40 p.m. Hymn: 'Just as I am, without one plea'

Prayer in pain

The Garden of Gethsemane: Luke 22.39–46.

After the brief respite in Bethany, the tension is really beginning to build up now.

If it is hard to let God love us, and learn to rest in his presence, it is even harder to love God when life goes bad on us. At times we are overwhelmed with suffering – the suffering of the world, our own personal pain, physical, mental, emotional, spiritual . . . 'What have I done to deserve this, why me?' we cry. 'God, where are you? Why don't you do something, put things right?'

And when we feel let down, betrayed, and cry out in our anger and bewilderment, Jesus in Gethsemane shows us where God is. Right there, suffering alongside us. 'Father, let this cup pass from me, yet not my will, but thine, be done.' God's will is not that people should suffer, but that people should live in wholeness and peace. Jesus absorbed all the hatred and pain without hitting back, so that that greater will of God could have its chance.

Prayer is not always sweet conversation – there are times when all we can do is speak through gritted teeth . . . Perhaps this silence won't be very comfortable, but we have to stay with it, as Jesus stayed with it in Gethsemane.

To ponder in the stillness

Save me, O God,
for the waters have come up to my neck.
I sink in deep mire, where there is no foothold;
I have come into deep waters, and the flood sweeps
over me.

Psalm 69.1–2

Silence

Poem: Psalm 84

Use this?
You must be joking.
Who could find comfort
In such bitter water?
Rather, let this cup
Pass from me,
This cannot be your will.
Why should life be
Like this?
Why me?

Why not?

And anyway,
There's not much choice.
It's this or nothing.
Use it for a well,
And see what happens.

In the heat of struggle
It is not sweetness which refreshes,
But the astringent bitterness
Which sets the teeth on edge.
Drink deep, and find
Mysterious refreshment.[5]

2.00 p.m. Hymn: 'Have faith in God, my heart'

Prayer at the cross

Jesus is crucified: Luke 23.33–34.

Now we stand at the foot of the cross. What do we make of it?

This is the point where prayer really searches us out, because Jesus said, 'If you want to be my disciple, this is where you must be – take up your cross and follow.'

We sometimes talk about unpleasant or difficult tasks or relationships as 'the cross we have to bear'. That trivializes the cross, and has more to do with Victorian piety than the gospel. The cross means being willing to join Jesus in acknowledging the hatred and evil that is all around us, and within us, too, when we are honest about it, and refusing to contribute to it or add to its power.

This is where we learn about forgiveness, about its cost. This is where to the outsider the Christian gospel looks like folly – but to those who believe, there is a touch of glory.

The motivation for taking up the cross is thanksgiving, not as punishment. It is our response to the amazing, forgiving love of God.

To ponder in the stillness

Bless the LORD, O my soul, and all that is within me,
bless his holy name.
Bless the LORD, O my soul, and do not forget all his benefits –
who forgives all your iniquity, who heals all your diseases.

Psalm 103.1–4

Silence

Poem: Rood-tree

I might have been his cradle,
Rocking him, folding
Securely against harm.
I could have been a ship,
Turning my sturdy timbers

To the wind, keeping him
Safe from storm.

Instead, they used me as
His cross.

No infant rages rocked the
Cradle tree, or storm lashed ship
Such as unleashed on me
That day. Shock waves of hatred
Crashed against me, bearing
On me through his body
Weight of world's pain,
Weight of his agony;
Wringing from him
Drop by drop,
'Why, God, you too?'

No comforting protection
Could I offer, or deliverance;
Only support, his mainstay in distress.

But did I hold him, or did he
With strength of purpose lovingly
Embrace his work of suffering,
Stretched on my arms?

They say it was a tree whose fruit
Brought sorrow to the world.
The fruit I bore,
Though seeming shame,
They call salvation.

My glory was it then
To be his tree.[6]

2.20 p.m. Hymn: 'When I survey the wondrous cross'

Prayer in darkness

'My God, My God, why have you forsaken me?' Matthew 27.46.

Here, at the heart of the mystery, is a sense of total loss. People have sometimes suggested that Jesus was saying Psalm 22, knowing that all would be well in the end. It seems to me that it is unlikely that in the extremity of pain and exhaustion, Jesus would be remembering anything as long as that Psalm. Once again, as with the thought of Jesus being angry, which we considered in connection with the cleansing of the Temple, perhaps we are saying more about ourselves than about Jesus. We don't want to let Jesus bear the agony of feeling abandoned by God, because we can't contemplate the possibility of that sort of pain.

But if that cry of desolation means anything to us at all, it must mean real desolation, desolation mirrored in the record of the event by the darkness that covered the earth. It means that we must not be surprised if what we experience at times, perhaps much of the time, is a feeling of God's absence, rather than a sense of his presence. Perhaps in retrospect, when we have been through a period of desolation, we can finish the Psalm, and say of the dark times, 'Yes, God was there too.' But in the middle of desolation, all we can do is hang on. Our prayer may not get further than, 'My God' – but that prayer is perhaps the most profound we shall ever pray.

To ponder in the stillness

My God, my God, why have you forsaken me?
Why are you so far from helping me, from the words
of my groaning?
O my God, I cry by day, but you do not answer;
and by night, but find no rest.

Psalm 22.1–2

Silence

Prayer (from Psalm 130)

Out of the deep we call to you, O Lord,
Lord, hear our prayer. **Amen.**

2.40 p.m. Hymn: 'O sacred head'

The prayer of trust

It is finished: John 19.30; Luke 23.46.

Our last session, at the foot of the cross, brings us to a settled place – the place where after all the agony and struggle, Jesus can say, 'It is finished.'

Not a thankful, 'That's over', but a recognition that he has accomplished what had to be done. In that knowledge, he can rest, trusting in God, 'Father, into your hands I commend my spirit.'

We have to learn that trust, that total surrender. We have to learn to trust, even when we're being crucified.

To ponder in the stillness

You who live in the shelter of the Most High,
who abide in the shadow of the Almighty,
will say to the Lord, 'My refuge and my fortress;
my God, in whom I trust.'

Psalm 91.1–2

Silence

Prayer

Keep us, good Lord,
under the shadow of your mercy
and, as you have bound us to yourself in love,
leave us not who call upon your name,
and grant us your salvation
made known in Jesus Christ our Lord. **Amen.**

2.56 p.m. Hymn: 'My song is love unknown' or 'Praise for the mighty love'

Conclusion

So we stand at the foot of the cross, where the battle has been lost and won. Humanly speaking, the last word lies with the centurion . . .

Poem: Crossroads

I cursed my luck, on duty in that heat:
The flies, the blood, the stench of death.
It was the loneliest place I've ever known,
Standing beside that cross. The crowds,
Hurling abuse, engulfed me with their hate;
Had he no friends? Standing not far away,
The women had more courage than the men,
But even his God, it seemed, had left him.
I've seen some crucifixions in my time,
But never one like this: the victim
More concerned for others than himself,
Asking forgiveness for his murderers.
And then that aweful darkness, when
The world died with him, and the cry that
Pierced the darkness pierced me too.
Did he say, 'Finished'? The way I feel
It's only just begun.[7]

Dismissal

And now we go out to continue the story.
In the name of Christ. Amen.

Notes

1. Anthony Bloom, *Courage to Pray*, Darton, Longman & Todd, 1973, p. 15.
2. *Watching for the Kingfisher*, p. 103.
3. Ibid., p. 13.
4. From 'Maundy Thursday', in *Watching for the Kingfisher*, p. 82.
5. *Watching for the Kingfisher*, p. 7.
6. Ibid., p. 86.
7. Ibid., p. 87.

Jesus on Easter Eve

In theory, this could be the shortest reflection in the series – on Easter Eve Jesus was safely in the tomb, wasn't he? That's what those who had crucified him thought, and that's what his disciples thought too.

> It was on the Saturday
> that he was not there
>
> From *Stages on the Way*[1]

It's hard for us who know how that weekend ended to get back to the sense of desolation experienced by the disciples, and the guilt some of them would have felt at having actively denied all knowledge of Jesus, left him to face his enemies alone. There must have been many 'if only's going through their minds – things could have been different if only . . . Two of them had particular reasons for feeling terrible. **Judas** put himself out of his misery:

> I thought he'd fight, I thought
> He would at last admit that
> I was right, the only way to
> Win Messiah's cause was by the
> Sword. He should have acted
> When they yelled 'Save now!'
> He could have overthrown them.
> I was wrong. My treacherous kiss
> Condemned both him and me:
> Him to a cross and me to
> Death of hope. My only course now
> Is to end it all.[2]

And so he did. **Peter** didn't take such drastic action, but he must have had a miserable time, going over the last few days:

What have I done? I who would
Never leave him, so I said.
What have I done? I slept
When he most needed company,
Denied I knew him when he
Needed friends, ran when
They led him to a cross,
Stayed distant in his suffering.
How can I bear the memory of his look,
The love accepting me as friend?
Master, what have I done?[3]

And there was nothing any of them could *do* because it was the Sabbath. Even the rituals which might have helped them grieve had to wait.

But there is an ancient tradition that says that Jesus wasn't safely in the tomb. We acknowledge it every time we say The Apostles Creed, in the statement, *he descended into hell*. At one level that can be taken to mean that he went to wherever dead spirits go. But there are two references in 1 Peter (3.18–20; 4.6) which suggest that Jesus went to the place of the departed with the definite purpose of rescuing them from the power of death, and bringing them to life with him.

In the Middle Ages, this was developed into a dramatic event, *The Harrowing of Hell*, 'Harrowing' is another way of saying 'harrying', a military term for making predatory raids. According to medieval theologians, Jesus went to Hades, trampled down its gates and rescued those who were imprisoned there, from Adam and Eve onwards from the power of Death. Death was overcome, as several of our Easter hymns proclaim. There is a hint in John's Gospel that Jesus would do this, where Jesus says to some of the Jews who were arguing with him, 'Truly I say to you, the hour is coming, and now is, when the dead will hear the voice of the Son of God, and those who hear will live . . . the hour is coming when all who are in the tombs will come forth, those who have done good to the resurrection of life, and those who have done evil to the resurrection of judgement' (John 5.25–9).

Perhaps even Judas was restored:

Judas restored

My road to hell was paved
With good intentions:
I thought he'd fight, and show them
He was king.
But I was wrong.
I couldn't live, knowing I had
Betrayed the one I loved. I thought
I'd have to bear that guilt for ever.
But I was wrong again.
No Sabbath rest for him:
He came in awesome power,
Trampled the gates of hell
And conquered Death, taking
All who were trapped in darkness
To live with him in everlasting light.
Purged by another kiss
He's set me free
To love him to eternity.[4]

People find it hard to make up their minds about Judas – not everyone can find it in their hearts to think that even he might be accepted into God's kingdom. When Laurence Whistler engraved a window for Moreton Church in Dorset, which showed Judas being drawn up to heaven by the rope with which he had hanged himself, with the thirty pieces of silver falling from his hand and turning into flowers as they reached the ground, although the PCC and the Diocesan

Advisory Committee accepted it, it was said that other local people refused to accept it, because they couldn't cope with the theological implication that it portrayed. (That window is not in the church with the other windows Whistler engraved, but in the local museum.) But if Jesus died for all, then just as the penitent thief was assured of a place in the Kingdom, there must be hope for the rest of us.

The descent into hell was a deliberate act, the completion of Christ's saving work – and the seal was set on its validity when God raised Jesus from the dead on Easter Day.

So Easter Eve wasn't a day when nothing happened, but a day of deep significance for our salvation.

Where will we be on Easter Eve? Just as it is hard to enter into the utter desolation felt by Jesus' friends at the time, it's hard to keep the stillness of that Sabbath. After all, we have much to do to prepare for the first day of the week. Ours is not preparation for a final act, but preparation for a new beginning. Let's savour the preparation, whether it's getting the church ready for a change of mood, or ourselves ready to renew our baptismal vows – or both – so that we will be able to enter into the joy that transformed life on that first Easter Day.

Notes

1. John Bell, *Stages on the Way*, Wild Goose Publications, 1998.
2. *Watching for the Kingfisher*, p. 84.
3. Ibid.
4. Ann Lewin, previously unpublished.

A simple vigil for Easter Eve

After lighting the new fire, and the Paschal candle, process into the church, lighting individual candles on the way.

Sing: 'The Lord is my light, my light and salvation,
In God I trust, in God I trust.' (Taizé)

When all the candles are lit, the ministry of the word begins:

Introduction

The first time God spoke, at creation, God said, 'Let there be light.' Tonight we come to give thanks for Jesus, the Light of the world, which the darkness of sin and death have not been able to overcome.

It is a long story, the story of our salvation. Year by year, we read in Scripture how God created men and women in his image, to live by his laws. We read how human beings chose to go their own way, with the consequent loss of their closeness to God and to each other.

We hear how God called his people with yearning love, again and again; how they responded and fell away. And God never let go. Sometimes, to save his people from disaster, God performed mighty acts, as with Noah, or at the parting of the waters of the Red Sea. Sometimes, individual prophets called the people back to God. At times, it seemed as though God's purpose would never be fulfilled, as his people were overpowered by foreign nations, and finally taken into exile. But there, at one of their lowest points, God spoke again with a message of new life.

Reading: Ezekiel 37.1–14.

Let us pause to reflect on God's faithfulness.

Silence, ending with

For all his mighty acts, and for his hidden mercies:
God's name be praised.

For keeping the word of hope alive through prophets and leaders:
God's name be praised.

For the promise of new life, when all seems hopeless and dead:
God's name be praised.

Hymn: 'The God of Abraham praise'

Restoration to their land did not bring total restoration of their relationship with God, though, and succeeding generations followed the pattern of turning to God and turning away again. Finally, as words did not seem to get through to his people, God performed his mighty act of deliverance in Jesus Christ. His life was an embodiment of God's word of love. His teaching and manner of life went right to the heart of what it means to live in close relationship with God. A tremendous struggle against the powers of darkness was focused on him, and, at one point, darkness appeared to have won. But out of the darkness came the voice of Jesus from the cross – 'It is finished. It is accomplished.'

On the third day, God's people began to understand what that cry from the cross meant, when Jesus, the Light which could not be overcome, appeared among them, risen from the dead.

Gospel: John 20.1–8.

Hymn: 'Now the green blade rises'

And the story goes on, for we have been called out of darkness to live in God's light. That is what our baptism means, and so it is most appropriate that on this night of thanksgiving, we should renew our vows.

Renewal of baptismal vows

Prayers, ending with the Lord's Prayer

Blessing

May the risen Lord Jesus watch over us and renew us as he renews the whole of creation. May our hearts and lives echo his love. **Amen.**

Sing: 'Kindle a flame' (Iona song)

Together we say

Lord Christ, set us on fire,
burn from us all that dims your light;
kindle an answering flame in lives around,
that darkness may be driven back
and glory stream into your world
transforming it with light. Amen.[1]

Note

1. From 'Candlemas Prayer', in *Watching for the Kingfisher*, p. 49.

A reflection for Easter Eve

At Christmas you probably heard the reading from St John's Gospel that describes the birth of Jesus in two ways. John called Jesus the Word of God made flesh, coming to live with us. He also spoke about the Light that enlightens everyone coming into the world, a light that shines in the darkness, and that cannot be extinguished (John 1.1–14).

When Jesus was preaching, you remember that he said, 'I am the light of the world. Whoever follows me will never walk in darkness, but will have the light of life' (John 8.12).

The events we were remembering in the early part of the week, and especially on Good Friday, showed how people tried very hard to extinguish the light. At one point it even looked as though they had succeeded, as darkness covered the earth, and Jesus died on the cross.

But the resurrection of Jesus, which we are beginning to celebrate, showed us that God isn't so easily defeated, and our Easter candle is our proclamation that Jesus is alive, and is the light for all people.

But Jesus didn't only say, 'I am the light of the world.' He also said to his followers, '*You* are the light of the world' . . . Let your light shine . . . so that [people] may give glory to your Father in heaven' (Matthew 5.14–16). Paul picked up this idea, too, when he wrote to the Christians at Ephesus (Ephesians 5.8–14): 'Once you were darkness, but now in the Lord you are light.' The Church reminds us of that in baptism, too, when the person who has been baptized is given a candle, and told to 'Shine as a light in the world, to the glory of God the Father'.

To take that to ourselves again, I invite you to give the light of Christ to each other as we light our candles from the light of the Paschal candle, saying as we pass the light on, 'The light of Christ'.

When the candles are lit

Often on Easter Eve, people renew their baptismal vows. These promises are about inviting Christ into our lives to drive out the darkness of sin, so that we can show Christ's light to the world.

We are invited to renew our promises now . . .

or

I invite you to join in the prayer:

Lord Christ, set us on fire,
burn from us all that dims your light;
kindle an answering flame in lives around,
that darkness may be driven back,
and glory stream into this world,
transforming it with light. Amen.[1]

We sing: 'The Spirit lives to set us free,
Walk, walk in the light'

At the end of the evening, take your candle with you, and light it again, tomorrow, and in the weeks ahead.

Note

1. From 'Candlemas Prayer', in *Watching for the Kingfisher*, p. 49.

A story of new life for Easter Day

Henry and Henrietta were two tiny, wriggly caterpillars. They lived on a bush in a beautiful garden, and every morning when they woke up, they began to eat the leaves of the bush. Occasionally, when they paused for a rest, they looked around them, and noticed that there were other creatures in the garden, too. Some wriggled along like they did, some hopped, some walked, some flew. Some were ugly, some were rather ordinary, some were beautiful to look at. But the most beautiful of all were the butterflies.

'Oh,' thought Henrietta, 'if only I could be a butterfly, beautiful and free.' She hadn't realized that she had spoken aloud, until a voice spoke from a nearby flower: 'You can be a butterfly, if you are willing to change.' Henrietta looked round to see who had spoken, and there, on the flower, rested a beautiful butterfly. 'I was like you once,' said the butterfly, gently fanning her wings, 'but I gave up being a wriggly caterpillar, so that I could become a butterfly, because that's what I was made for.'

'Is it hard?' asked Henrietta. 'Not very,' said the butterfly. 'When the time is right for you to start to change, you'll find that you can spin a cocoon to protect you while you grow. It's not hard, but you will feel as though you are dead for a while, until new life begins to stir.'

'Did you hear that?' Henrietta said to Henry. 'We can be beautiful, free butterflies.'

'Sounds a bit risky to me,' said Henry. 'I'm happy as I am, munching these leaves, and getting bigger and fatter. You do what you like, but I'm going to be the biggest and best caterpillar there has ever been.' And he went on eating.

Nothing Henrietta said could make him change his mind. She was sad about that, because she enjoyed his company, and would have liked to share this rather scary adventure with him.

Sure enough, one day Henrietta thought it was the right

time to make a start. She discovered that, as the butterfly had said, two of her legs had a special ability to spin thread, and she began to cover her body with it, round and round, until nothing could be seen of her old caterpillar shape. It was very dark and a bit scary. She began to wonder if she'd done the right thing. Perhaps Henry had been right after all, and it would have been better to stay as a caterpillar, and try to be the biggest caterpillar there had ever been. But she'd done it now. She would never get out of this cocoon alive. She would never see Henry again.

But just as she reached the depths of despair, she began to feel something happening around her. Her cocoon was breaking open, light was coming in, and warmth. She began to stretch – and found that in the darkness she had grown wings. In the warmth of the sun, she began to move them up and down, and discovered that she could fly. 'It's true,' she shouted in delight, 'I'm a butterfly – I am beautiful – this is what I was meant to be.'

Meanwhile, Henry was very uncomfortable. His skin was tight, and he found it hard to move. He wished he'd never said he wanted to be the biggest and best caterpillar there ever was. And he was lonely without Henrietta, too – life didn't seem to make sense any more. He felt awful, and very sorry for himself.

But then he heard a voice that he knew, calling him. 'Henry!' He looked round, thinking that Henrietta had come back. But all he could see was a beautiful butterfly, gently fanning her wings beside him. 'Henry,' the voice said again. 'It's me, Henrietta.

It's true, it's worth the risk. Don't try and cling on to your old way of life. Come through the darkness, and join me in the light of this new life.'

So Henry had his chance after all, and he and Henrietta danced in sunlight for the rest of their lives.

We heard another story this morning when someone was told not to cling on to an old way of understanding: the story of Mary Magdalene in the garden, looking for the body of

Jesus. She was told that she was looking for the wrong thing, because Jesus was not dead, but risen.

As we've followed Jesus from his entry into Jerusalem on Palm Sunday, through the growing tension of his encounters with various people in authority, as well as the illumination of his encounters with his followers, we've thought a lot during this week how we are continually being invited to let old ways die, so that new life can come. Everything led up to the cross on Good Friday, that very dark, scary place. And now this glorious day of the resurrection comes to us again, with the same message:

> If you have been raised with Christ, seek the things that are above, where Christ is, seated at the right hand of God. Set your minds on things that are above, not on things that are on earth.
>
> Colossians 3.1–2

Listen to Jesus saying

> 'Do not cling . . .
> Let me be bigger than your
> Heart can hold.
> Rise with me to a
> Larger vision.'[1]

The Lord is risen, he is risen indeed. Alleluia!

Note

1. From 'Easter Morning', in *Watching for the Kingfisher*, p. 88.

Intercessions for Easter Day

Very early in the morning on that first day of the week, new life was born. With Christians throughout the world, we thank you, Father, for the resurrection of your Son. We thank you for all the signs of new life in the natural world; for signs of new life in places where the future seemed hopeless, and we pray for people still entombed in the darkness of oppression and hatred, where life struggles to be born against the odds. Lord, roll away the stones of obstinacy and anger, and let your life bring peace and hope.
Life-giving God, **hear our prayer.**

We pray for the church, that we will be signs of life and hope in our world. Like the beloved disciple, may we all stay close enough to you to hear the heartbeat of your will, and discern where life is to be found. When we fail to recognize you, call us by name, as you called Mary, and assure us of your presence in our daily lives. We pray for all church leaders seeking the truth from different standpoints, and for us all in our witness to your risen life. Roll away the stones that prevent us from moving on, and let your life open us up to new possibilities.
Life-giving God, **hear our prayer.**

We pray for the communities we belong to, and give thanks for our neighbours and friends. We pray for all who are lonely. God of all people, roll away the stones that keep us apart, and let your love draw us closer together as we draw closer to you.
Life-giving God, **hear our prayer.**

We thank you, risen Lord, for the stirrings of resurrection in our own lives. We pray for all who feel a long way from resurrection because of illness, anxiety, bereavement.

Space for our own prayers, or to name those we carry on our hearts

Roll away the stones of doubt and fear, Lord, and help us all to open ourselves to your gift of life.
Life-giving God, **hear our prayer.**

We thank you for the hope that the Resurrection brings. We pray for all approaching death, and for those who watch with them and care for them. We give thanks for all who have gone before us on this journey through death to life, and we pray that with them we will be given a share in your eternal kingdom.
Life-giving God, **accept our prayers for the sake of your Risen Son. Amen.**

Eucharistic Prayer for Easter

Lord God,
through your Son, Jesus Christ,
you have renewed our hope
in life that cannot be destroyed by death.
We thank you for calling us
to witness to the resurrection:
Lord, keep us faithful.

With Mary Magdalene, Peter, John
and all who through the ages have believed
although they have not seen,
we join the angels and archangels
and all the company of heaven, as we sing:
Holy, holy, holy Lord,
God of life and love,
heaven and earth are full of your glory,
all praise to your name.

Accept our praises now, Lord God,
as we remember Jesus, who,
the night before he died,
took bread and wine, gave you thanks
and offered them to his friends, saying,
'This is my body, this is my blood.
Eat and drink to remember me.'

In joy and awe we stand before you,
and proclaim:
Dying he destroyed our death,
rising he restored our life.
Lord Jesus, come in glory.

Come freshly to us, living God:
open our eyes
that we may recognize you walking with us;
open our ears and our minds
that we may hear and understand;
open our hearts
that your love may flow through us
and bring the blessing of new life
to all we meet;
for you are the God who makes all things new.

Blessing and honour and glory and power be yours for ever and ever. Amen.

Ascension Day

When I was a child, Ascension Day was always a special day, a holiday at the school I attended, a golden day, full of glory.

One day seems very much like another now, even Sunday can be spent just like the rest. Our sense of the rhythm of the year belonging to the Christian story has gradually been diminished. Public holidays have had a major shift ever since Harold Wilson's government moved the Whitsun holiday to the end of May, instead of celebrating it inconveniently as a movable feast attached to the Christian Pentecost, which, of course, depends on the date of Easter. Holiday has become a secular word, far removed from its origin in 'holy day'. But, however we spend it, Ascension Day is a special day in the Christian calendar, a day which marks the completion of the story of Jesus' earthly life, though not the end of his relationship with us.

The ascension is a puzzling event if we try to take it too literally. It is recorded in language which belongs to a different era, when people didn't understand the shape of the universe or, rather, thought it had a very clearly defined shape. The earth was flat, and surrounded by water. Over it the sky fitted like a dome, and above the dome was heaven where God was to be found. Two thousand years on, we've discovered a lot about our physical surroundings. We know that the sky isn't solid. Yuri Gagarin, the first Russian cosmonaut, told us that he didn't find God or heaven when he went into space. We know that the earth isn't flat – it's all much more complex than people ever imagined.

And language is complex too. We talk about things being 'up' or 'down' without giving the words any sense of direction. Each year at school, I 'went up' to a new class at the beginning of September. Sometimes that actually meant moving down a floor in the building. If we are 'put down' by someone, we are devalued, not moved a couple of feet lower. Our language in many ways reflects that old picture of the universe. So moving on to something richer and fuller is symbolized by the word 'up'. And we are using language in that symbolic way when we talk about the ascension. Just as at Christmas we sang, 'He came down to earth from heaven, who is God and Lord of all', now at the ascension we sing about the completion of that earthly, incarnate life, and celebrate with our upbeat language (there we go again!) the lordship of Christ over all creation.

'Lord' is another word we have to work at – it doesn't sit comfortably with our twenty-first-century view of things. Some would like to get rid of lords altogether. But it goes further than a feeling that it's unfair to inherit power and land. We've spoilt the word and the concept by the way some of us 'lord it' over others. All through human history, people have misused their power and abused those whom they were supposed to protect.

But Jesus gave the word 'lord' a special meaning. He said to the disciples (Mark 10.42–45) 'You know that among the Gentiles those whom they recognize as their rulers lord it over them . . . but it is not so among you . . . whoever wishes to be first among you must be slave of all.' And he gave them a particular demonstration of what he meant when he washed their feet: 'You call me Teacher and Lord,' he said, 'and you are right, for that is what I am' (John 13.13), but I don't lord it over you, I respect you and accept you as you are, feet and all. And that is how you must treat one another. Real humility does not lie in thinking we are no good. It lies in looking at others and recognizing their value – we could even say 'looking up to them'.

Washing people's feet is not a way of making them more acceptable. It is a way of taking people as we find them, sore and weary or fresh and dancing, and seeking to serve them, whatever their need. It's not so much that we have something to give them, as recognizing that all our fellow humans are special to God, just as we are. Washing their feet, in whatever form that takes, will help them to realize that too.

We are always being asked to choose whether we will join Christ in service or not. The Lordship of Christ does not speak of a remote being, distant from all our concerns, but about an involved God who wants his kingdom to be established. God longs for justice where there is injustice, sufficiency where there is poverty, health where there is sickness, knowledge where there is ignorance. And we are the people he has called to work with him to bring his kingdom nearer.

If that seems a rather big undertaking, way beyond our grasp, remember the promise Jesus gave: 'You will receive power when the Holy Spirit has come upon you, and you will be my witnesses' (Acts 1.8) and 'I am sending upon you what my Father promised; so stay here in the city until you have been clothed with power from on high' (Luke 24.49).

So we're not expected to do God's work *for* him, but *with* him, in his strength, filled with his Spirit – a kind of divine job-share. May the Spirit open us up and transform us, so that we will be able to live the good news we have to share.

Intercessions for Ascension Day

Risen and ascended Lord, we rejoice and give you thanks for your victory over sin and death, and for the new life you give us. Fill us with your Spirit, that we may share the good news in every aspect of our lives.
Lord, in your mercy, **hear our prayer.**

Lord of the world, give your grace to all who exercise authority, whether they recognize you or not. We pray for all leaders that they may use their power with compassion and justice. May we all be influences for good, and bring your kingdom nearer.
Lord, in your mercy, **hear our prayer.**

Lord of the Church, we pray for all who have particular responsibilities as leaders. We pray that where we disagree with each other, we will learn to listen with courtesy, and act in charity. Help us all to be faithful to you in our response to your call, so that our witness may draw others to worship you.
Lord, in your mercy, **hear our prayer.**

Lord Christ, you promised to be with us always. We thank you for our families and friends, through whom in part your love is made known. We pray for our local communities, and for all who find it hard to believe in your love, whose circumstances are overshadowed by poverty or lack of food. We pray that all who work to improve the lives of others will know your presence with them. Move us all to deeper generosity in response to your love.
Lord, in your mercy, **hear our prayer.**

Lord of wholeness, we bring to you all who suffer in body, mind or spirit, especially those we carry on our hearts . . . .
Lord, give us all the healing that we need.
Lord, in your mercy, **hear our prayer.**

We pray for all who have died: those whose faith was obvious, and those whose faith was known to you alone. May we with all your saints in this life and the next, be raised up to share with you in glory.
Lord, in your mercy, **hear our prayer.**

The Ascension and mission

'Go therefore and make disciples of all nations' (Matthew 28.19). At Ascensiontide it is hard to avoid thinking about the meaning of mission, because that is what the gospel calls us to. Our spiritual growth is not something we engage in for our own benefit, or so that people will think how wonderful we are. Our aim has to be that people will learn how wonderful God is in his transforming grace (Matthew 5.16). Although Matthew's Gospel was directed to Jewish people, he did not forget that the Jewish mission was to all the nations (Isaiah 49.6). At the beginning of the Gospel, the nations come to Christ, in the persons of the Magi. At the end, the disciples are sent out to all nations. The Church is to be the new Israel.

So we come to the question: 'What is mission?' And how do we do it? That command to go out and make disciples of all nations was the spur for missionary work throughout the centuries, and some of it was done from rather questionable motives – not all Church history bears too close an examination. In the nineteenth century, it was the driving force behind the work of missionary societies from this country, which sent people out to what they thought of as the benighted parts of the world, to bring people to the light. In the twentieth century, as the British Empire crumbled, questions began to be asked about how far spreading the Christian gospel had been part of Empire building, part of the package that imposed the British way of life, rather than a desire to help people see God as he is in Jesus. Christian mission must always be fuelled by that desire.

We are faced with real questions, though, about how we relate to people of different faith traditions. Attitudes have changed over the last 50 years or so, as we've learnt more about the ancient traditions of other cultures and learnt to respect them, and to appreciate the insights they have into the nature of God. This change is reflected sometimes in the hymns we sing, or don't sing. As a teenager I used to go to missionary meetings, where often one of the hymns chosen as part of the worship was 'From Greenland's icy mountains . . .' which listed all the places where the light of Christ had never been seen, and contained the words, 'The heathen in his blindness bows down to wood and stone'. You won't find words like that in hymns now, even if you can find the hymns.

In the hymn, 'Thy kingdom come, O God', the words of one verse, 'O'er heathen lands afar, thick darkness broodeth yet', have been changed to 'O'er lands both near and far . . .' Thirty years ago when I was teaching in Sheffield, we sang the unreconstructed version – political correctness hadn't come into fashion then. I remember standing in church as we sang it, with my thoughts travelling about six miles to the outer city estate where I taught, an estate with huge problems caused by deprivation. The darkness seemed pretty impenetrable there. And in the school community there were two faith groups, some Christians fairly sure they were right, and a group of Muslim lads who put many Christians to shame by their steady witness to the importance of their faith. This was pointed up very sharply one year when Ramadan coincided with Lent in a very snowy February. As most of us, Christians and all, rushed towards hot chocolate and the KitKat machine at break-time, when the rule was that pupils had to go outside, the Muslims simply asked if they could be allowed to stay in the building because they found it hard to cope with the cold when they were fasting. They were fasting to show their love for God. How did the Christians show their love? It was quite a challenge.

When I came back to Southampton 25 years ago, I was involved with the early inter-faith explorations in the city, and I found myself challenged again by the experience of meeting people of different faiths – but this time on their own terms. Standing in the Hindu temple, looking at the images of the gods, all my colonial prejudices rose up – the heathen, blindness, bowing down to wood and stone. And then almost like a physical blow I was struck by the question: You say that you believe in one God, what does that mean? Could it be that God has different ways of revealing himself in different cultures? Sitting in a Sikh Gurdwara, where I didn't understand a word of what was going on, I had a strong sense that it was God who was being worshipped. Meeting Muslims in their place of worship wasn't possible then – they were a tiny community meeting in a house adapted for the purpose, and there was only room for the men to pray together. But we were invited to go to meet them out of worship hours, and we talked with one Muslim who said more than once that the purpose of our conversations must always be to make us better members of our own faith community.

It is not easy. When we hold convictions, they matter. But our convictions can be sharpened and deepened by exploring the convictions of others and offering them the insights of our own, not to demolish their arguments, but for mutual enrichment. For some people, truth is like a castle: once you have got into it, you are safe. But you have to defend it from attack and, in effect, it can become your prison. For other people, truth is more like a journey, with camps pitched along the way, where pilgrims meet each other and exchange ideas. This kind of exchange challenges us to discover what we really mean when we say, 'Jesus is Lord.'

One of the things I have realized is that we hear things in a certain way because we've always heard them that way. For example, an often-used text in inter-faith discussions is, 'No one comes to the Father but by me.' The emphasis is always put on *me*. Why should it not be on *Father*? There is nothing in the Greek from which that verse is translated to say where the emphasis should fall. And to emphasize 'Father' opens up other possibilities. John Hick put this helpfully when he wrote:

> No-one comes to the Father – that is to God as Father – except through Christ, in whom as Son the love of the Father is fully revealed. But millions of men and women may in Buddhism have come to God as release out of suffering into Nirvana; or in Islam to God as sovereign and holy will addressing the Arab peoples through Mohammed; or in Hinduism to God as many-sided source and meaning of life. And further, it may be that Christ (as personal love) is also present in these other religions, and their several awarenesses of God likewise present to some extent in Christianity.[1]

For Christians, the special uniqueness of Jesus is that he shows the character and nature of God the Father as only a Son can. He focuses all the other insights we have about the nature of God. But it is worth remembering that much of the proclamation in the New Testament is about the Christ who is to come – we haven't got all the truth in our grasp yet. I'm sure it's true that in Christ 'all the fullness of God was pleased to dwell' (Colossians 1.19). But I'm not sure we fully understand yet what that means.

The alternative to dialogue, the attempt to get to know and understand, is the fanaticism which tries to impose our way on others, the attitude which the 2004 Reith Lecturer, Wole Soyenka, described as the 'I'm right, you're dead' approach, with which we have become all too familiar.

Mission, the dialogue which includes listening, has to begin from the place of humility. That is what the incarnation demonstrated. Dialogue has to leave room for people to disagree without destroying each other. If we really believe there is one God, we have nothing to fear from people who understand God differently. God is much greater than any human, or religion, can comprehend, and God will draw people to respond to him in the ways he wants. Our job as Christians is to witness to how God is in Jesus, and we can leave the rest to God. We can trust the promise Jesus gave us: 'You will know the truth.' He didn't go on to say 'and the truth will keep you safe', but 'the truth will make you free' (John 8.32).

Note

1. Quoted by John Robinson in the chapter 'The Uniqueness of Christ', in his book *Truth is Two-Eyed*, SCM Press, 1979, p. 107.

Pentecost

'What's going on?' That seems to have been the question on everyone's lips at Pentecost. The reason for the question is clear when we read the account of that day in Acts 2. The Christians were gathered together, and suddenly a violent wind swept through the house, and tongues of flame rested on each person there, and the Holy Spirit filled them. They were so excited that they spilled out into the street, talking at the tops of their voices. The extraordinary thing was that everyone who heard them understood as though it was their own language being spoken, whatever country they came from. 'What does it mean? What's going on?' they said.

Some people dismissed the whole affair as drunken revelry, but Peter brought them down to earth. Apart from the fact that it was the wrong time of day for drunkenness, he told the crowd that they ought to recognize that this was what was foretold by the prophets. He quoted one called Joel, who had said that God promised to pour out God's Spirit on everyone, young, old, male and female, and the result would be outward signs of excitement and disturbance, and inwardly the opening up of the possibility of salvation, of being changed (Joel 2. 28–32).

Peter could have pointed to other clues which were there in the events: the people who were wondering what was happening would all have known their Scriptures. They would have known that the word for 'wind' or 'breath' was a word that also meant 'spirit'. They would have remembered that Ezekiel had seen the dry bones of the Jewish people revived by the Spirit of God (Ezekiel 37.1–14). They would have known, too, that fire was a sign of God's presence: ever since the time that Moses heard God speaking from the middle of the burning bush, flame had carried that symbolism. But perhaps those people present at Pentecost were like us, knowing things in our heads, but a bit slow to make the connection between what we know intellectually, and what we experience.

So what was going on, and what might it mean for us today? We could perhaps pick up a different clue. John recalled at the beginning of his Gospel (John 3.1–8) how Jesus had said to Nicodemus, 'You must be born again, filled with God's Spirit.' Again, as with Hebrew, the Greek word for 'wind' is the same as that for 'spirit'. Jesus went on to talk about the mysterious way the wind operates, blowing where it wants to. We don't know where it has come from or where it is going. We may understand more about weather systems now than people in first-century Palestine, but we are no nearer to being able to control the wind. No more are we able to control God's Spirit.

Some of the things we say about the wind may help us to understand more about the way the Spirit of God will affect us. We talk about an idea or a person coming like a breath of fresh air: blowing away the cobwebs, clearing the air. So God's Spirit can set us free from habits and ways of thinking that keep us stuck, and prevent us from seeing straight. And we talk about 'the wind of change', too. That's more radical than simply feeling a breath of fresh air. It's the phrase that came into prominence in the 1960s, when the first signs appeared that apartheid in South Africa was beginning to crack up. And that process meant real upheaval, painful change which is still going on.

So, when Jesus said that the Spirit would come and lead us into truth (John 16.13), he was not just talking about the Spirit sorting out our muddled thinking. He was saying that there is real, hard work to be done. Repentance, turning round to face the truth, is costly. And the Spirit of God gives us the clarity to see, and the energy to do, what needs to be done.

For the other attribute of wind that can help us is its energy. We are getting used to the idea of wind-farms providing us with power. But the energy of the wind isn't just for work, the wind can set things dancing, too: it's there to be enjoyed and played with, especially if we're lucky enough to have a kite to fly. The Spirit of God can set *us* dancing, too, filling us with joy in the fullness of life which Jesus said he had come to bring.

Jeu d'Esprit

Flame-dancing Spirit, come,
Sweep us off our feet and
Dance us through our days.
Surprise us with your rhythms,
Dare us to try new steps, explore
New patterns and new partnerships.
Release us from old routines
To swing in abandoned joy
And fearful adventure.
And in the intervals,
Rest us,
In your still centre.[1]

Note

1. *Watching for the Kingfisher*, p. 91.

Intercessions for Pentecost

Creator God, we thank you for the gift of your Spirit, and for calling us to be members of your church. As we take our place among the witnesses to your love, we pray that you will keep us faithful to our calling.
Come freshly to us, Spirit of God, **bring life, and hope and truth.**

Lord God, we thank you for the rich variety of your gifts. Help us to discover and use our gifts, and to rejoice in the gifts of others.
Come freshly to us, Spirit of God, **bring life, and hope and truth.**

Spirit of peace, we thank you for all who work for peace. We pray for all who are at war with each other, and for those suffering the consequences of war. We pray for all trying to rebuild communities.
Come freshly to us, Spirit of God, **bring life, and hope and truth.**

God of wisdom, we thank you for all good government, and pray for all in positions of authority, in religious and secular life throughout the world. May we all use the influence we have for the good of all.
Come freshly to us, Spirit of God, **bring life, and hope and truth.**

God of wholeness, we thank you for our health. We pray for all in need of any kind, that they will know your sustaining presence with them.
In a few moments of quiet we bring before you the people and situations we carry on our hearts . . . .
Lord, we pray that you will give us all the healing that we need.
Come freshly to us, Spirit of God, **bring life, and hope and truth.**

God of time and eternity, we thank you for the lives of all who have encouraged us and taught us of your love, and now live in your fuller presence. We pray that we in turn will be given a share in your glory.
Father, we pray in the power of your Spirit that you will accept our prayers for the sake of Jesus, your Son. **Amen.**

Eucharistic Prayer for Pentecost

Eternal God:
We praise you for your glory.

We praise you that in Jesus,
now risen and glorified,
you offer us fullness of life
beyond our imagining:
Raise us to life with him.

We praise you for the Spirit's
disturbing presence, urging us on
to explore the riches of your love:
Open our hearts to your transforming power.

Open us up to your glory, Lord, as
with angels and archangels, and
all who have responded to your call,
we praise you, saying:
Holy, holy, holy Lord,
God of power and joy,
heaven and earth are full of your glory,
all praise to your name.

Be with us now, Lord God,
as we remember Jesus, who
the night before he died,
took bread and wine, blessed them,
and gave them to his friends, saying,
'This is my body given for you.
This is my blood, shed for you.
Eat and drink to remember me.'

Come freshly to us, living God,
as we share these holy gifts.
Flame-dancing Spirit come:
Sweep us off our feet and
dance us through our days.

Surprise us with your rhythms:
Dare us to try new steps, explore
new patterns and new partnerships.

Release us from old routines:
To swing in abandoned joy
and fearful adventure.

And in the intervals:
Rest us in your still centre. Amen.

Section 3

Ordinary Time

Ordinary Time

All the excitement is over for another year in terms of the Church's calendar. For half the year, the calendar gives us a framework within which to pray and live. It starts with Advent, a time of waiting, if we can manage it with all the competing commercial and domestic preparations for Christmas. Then there's the celebration of God coming into the world in human form. We're caught up in the wonder of it all, we hear the angels' song and marvel at the variety of visitors to the newborn child. We watch his parents go through the processes required by the Law when they present him to God in the Temple. Then, after a brief pause, we are plunged into Lent, Holy Week, Good Friday, Easter, the Ascension and Pentecost. There's so much to take in that, though we repeat the cycle every year, we always seem to find new truths to reflect on, new depths to the love of God.

And on the day after Pentecost, the Church's calendar says in small type, 'Ordinary Time resumes today.' There are no major festivals between Pentecost and Advent except for Trinity: God in all God's mystery and wonder. That's all we've got, and all we need. As Julian of Norwich said, 'In God we have all.'

And it's 'Ordinary Time', the name given to the parts of the year when there are no major fasts or feasts to be observed, only God. We hardly noticed the other period of Ordinary Time, a few weeks between the Presentation in the Temple and the beginning of Lent. Now we've got six months, the long green season of Trinity. But it's not six months for doing nothing in particular: green, the liturgical colour for the season, is also the colour we associate with growth. So we've got six months to digest all that we received in the earlier period of intense attention to God's activity in Jesus, six months to learn what it means to live in the power of the Spirit, six months to wonder at the splendour and mystery of God, six months of good growing time before we take ourselves into the new cycle and new discoveries about God and ourselves.

When you think about it, 'Ordinary Time' is a strange term, because whatever else time is, it is hardly 'ordinary'. Time is a great mystery. It does funny things. Or perhaps it is our attitude to time, rather than time itself, which is odd. We say that we have 24 hours in every day, but sometimes we wonder where time has gone. We run out of it, we waste it, we kill it, or it hangs heavy for us. We make time when we want to do something, we buy time when we're not sure what to do, we mark time when we're waiting, we save time (but never seem to be able to find the time we've saved when we want it), we say we haven't got time when we want to get out of something.

The ordered division of time into days, hours, minutes, is what we have developed in order for society to operate. Musicians know about that: if they want to play together, one of the first things they have to learn is to keep time. But people have very different attitudes to time: some are bound by it, always punctual, never missing deadlines; others are much more casual. There are cultural differences of approach too: our western preoccupation with time is viewed with amusement or exasperation by people in other parts of the world – 'You have clocks,' they say, 'we have time.'

Now we have time. Time to let what we have learnt take root, and come to fruition in our lives. The truth of the incarnation is that God meets us in time, in the events and encounters of daily life. The Bible talks about time in different ways. There is 'chronos', clock time, and there is 'kairos', the judgement time, the time when God breaks into clock time, and we either recognize him or we miss him, rather like the woman and Simon the Pharisee in the encounter recorded in the Gospel (Luke 7.36–50). The woman responded to God in Jesus, but Simon dismissed him as not worth the ordinary courtesies of hospitality, almost as though, in spite of having invited him for a meal, he didn't want to give him the time of day.

God is always stepping into our ordinary time, challenging and surprising us into new awareness. We don't have to wait until Advent comes round again to learn to be alert, to keep awake, to remind ourselves to look for the signs of God's coming in the things that we do, the people we meet. We've got time to grow and be nourished by God's gifts: to be strengthened in faith, built up in hope and grow in love; and all for the sake of Jesus Christ, our Lord.

Eucharistic Prayer for daily life

Creator God, in whose design
joy and woe are woven together,
we thank you for calling us
to work with you in weaving
the fabric of your kingdom.

We thank you that
in your Son Jesus Christ,
you have given us a pattern for ministry,
and that yoked with him
in joys and sorrows
we have strength for the task.

Be with us now
as we remember Jesus,
who, on the night before he died,
took bread and wine, blessed them
and gave them to his friends, saying,
'This is my body, given for you.
This is my blood, shed for you.
Eat and drink to remember me.'

Come freshly to us now, Lord God,
and in the midst of struggle keep us
joyful in hope.
Pour out your Holy Spirit as we
bring before you these gifts and
remember Christ's sacrifice
made once for all on the cross.
Feed us with his body and blood
that we may live and grow in him.

Pick up the threads of our experience;
craft your pattern in us and through us,
and in your time reveal its significance;
for you are the God who
weaves the opportunities of our daily lives,
our joys and sorrows,
into the glory of your eternal kingdom. **Amen.**

Trinity Sunday

You have probably heard the story about the church where on Trinity Sunday, as the Book of Common Prayer requires, the congregation was reciting the Athanasian Creed, with its rolling statements: 'The Father incomprehensible, the Son incomprehensible and the Holy Spirit incomprehensible . . .'; and a crochety voice from the pews said, 'If you ask me, the whole darned thing is incomprehensible.'

And that's what Trinity Sunday is all about. God *is* incomprehensible, far beyond our understanding, greater by far than our imagining.

We've spent half the Christian year learning about God's dealings with his people. Year by year, we read in Scripture how God created women and men in his own image, to live by his laws. We have heard again how human beings chose to go their own way with the consequent loss of their closeness to God and each other. But God never gave up on them. Over and over again, God called his people with yearning love; and over and over again, people responded and then fell away. And, at last, God spoke in a living word, Jesus, the embodiment of God's love. We have heard his words, and seen his way of life, which go right to the heart of what it means to live in close relationship with God. We watched the struggle with the powers of evil focused on the cross. We saw apparent defeat turned round again by a mighty act of God in the resurrection. We kept company with Christ during the great 40 days as he opened the Scriptures to people who had missed the point. We acknowledged the end of his earthly ministry at the ascension, and we waited with eager anticipation for the coming of the Spirit at Pentecost. So our experience has been of God as Father, Son and Holy Spirit: Creator, Redeemer and Sanctifier.

And then comes Trinity Sunday, and we realize that we don't understand, and that perhaps in this life we never will, because there is always more. We cannot define God, because any definition limits God to what our human minds can hold. And always there is more. Jesus said that the Spirit would lead us into truth (John 16.13). Discovering God is a journey.

Those who tried to describe God in Scripture often had difficulty in finding the right words. Think of Ezekiel. In his attempt to describe his vision of God (Ezekiel 1) he couldn't get any closer than repeatedly saying, 'there was something like . . .'. And he ended with the words, 'This was the appearance of the likeness of the glory of God.' His response was to fall down in worship. The same response is called out in a very similar vision recorded in Revelation 4. The vision of God calls us to worship. 'You are worthy, our Lord and God, to receive glory and honour and power, for you created all things, and by your will they existed and were created' (Revelation 4.11).

Of course, we must look for ways of expressing our understanding of God, so that we can share our good news. But we must never think that we can define God. Scripture teaches us that the appropriate response to coming closer to God is worship. Worship takes us beyond our definitions, and brings us closer to poetry than to prose.

Trinity Sunday reminds us that God is a God who continually surprises us into fresh understanding. And yet there is more.

Eucharistic Prayer for Trinity

(with *Peruvian Gloria*)[1]

Blessed are you, Lord God,
that you are always and only God:
Blessed are you, Lord God.

Blessed are you, Lord God,
that you have revealed yourself
in Jesus Christ:
Blessed are you, Lord God.

Blessed are you, Lord God,
for you lead us to know you
through your Spirit:
Blessed are you, Lord God.

Holy God, vulnerable and strong,
we praise and bless you,
and with all who adore you
in earth and heaven, we sing:

Glory to God, Glory to God, Glory to the Father
Glory to God, Glory to God, Glory to the Father
To God be glory for ever
To God be glory for ever
Alleluia, Amen. **Alleluia, Amen; Alleluia, Amen.**

Glory to God, Glory to God, Glory to Christ Jesus
(Repeat as above)

Glory to God, Glory to God, Glory to the Spirit
(Repeat as above)

All praise and glory be to you, Lord God,
as we remember Jesus, who
the night before he died,
took bread and wine, blessed them
and gave them to his friends, saying,
'This is my body, this is my blood.
Eat and drink to remember me.'

Come freshly to us now, Lord God,
and fill us with your grace.

May our hearts overflow with love for you,
our spirits dance with joy in you,
our wills be drawn by desire for you;
for you have called us
to be your friends, and live
to your praise and glory. Amen.[1]

Note

1. One source of the *Peruvian Gloria*, which is in the public domain, is *The Wee Worship Book* (fourth incarnation), Wild Goose Worship Group, 1999, p. 116.

Leading a balanced life – the advantage of having a Rule

The idea of a Rule of Life does not sit easily in the vocabulary of many people today. But we probably all have one. There are things we do as a rule which keep us healthy: we eat, drink and wash. We work (taking that in its broadest sense, not just the gainful employment aspect) and we know that for the sake of our health and sanity we need recreation and holidays, and an appropriate amount of sleep. So, as a rule, we have meals at regular times, we go to bed at a similar time most days, and get up at a similar time most mornings. This rule does not imprison us – if we need to be up very early one day, we might go to bed a bit earlier the night before. If we have a late night, we sleep in the next day. If we're camping in the wilds perhaps we don't wash as often as when we have water on tap. Our pattern of life can be flexible, but we are mostly glad of a routine which sustains us. The decisions we make about the routine mean that we don't have to waste energy deciding every day about things which we know are necessary to our health.

The same principle applies in our spiritual life too. We know that for our spiritual health there are things we need to do and the language is important. We perhaps began doing things because we were told we *ought* to, but until we recognize the *need* we don't take them on for ourselves. We had to learn, when we were little, about eating sensibly, about washing regularly (especially the bits we didn't think anyone could see), about adequate rest. As we grew up these things became natural, even desirable. I often think, as I hear a child protesting about bedtime, that it won't be long before, like many adults, that child will be thankful to be able to go to bed!

We seem to take a little longer to get to spiritual maturity. We need a reminder to help us to live a balanced life. And that's where a Rule of Life comes in. We decide what the essential elements of life are, and how we are going to give them proper attention. Making a decision about personal prayer, joining in public worship, a simple lifestyle, use of money, recreation, proper time with family and friends, saves us having to reinvent our plan every day, helps us to prioritize what we need, and ensures that we don't leave important elements of our inner life to chance.

Benedict, who lived in the sixth century, was responsible for the Rule which became the foundation of monastic life in its various forms. Prayer was at the centre of his Rule: the monks and nuns met seven times a day for corporate worship. The rest of the time was divided between work, study and rest. His Rule provided for an ordered and balanced life, where all people from the apparently most important to the seemingly unimportant were to be treated with respect; where food and drink were to be provided so that no one was in want; where all tools and clothing were to be looked after, and all in the context of learning to find God in all things. 'Prefer nothing to the love of Christ' is the requirement at the heart of the Rule. But it is not a straitjacket, it's a guide.

A Rule of Life helps us to keep our balance amid all the demands made on us. It reminds us that prayer is the foundation of the whole of our life, it is our relationship with God in action. So our commitment to God is worked out in the way we live, how we love our neighbour and how we love ourselves. Paying attention to our need for rest and recreation will make us more available to others, and including in our care for others concern for the resources of the created world will ensure that we reflect God's delight in all that is.

Benedict encouraged discipline, but he required it to be practised with a certain lightness of touch. Monks were enjoined quietly (for this was during Greater Silence) to encourage one another as they arose for the Night Office, 'for the sleepy like to make excuses' (Ch. 22 of the *Rule*). All were expected to be in their places in chapel at the latest by the end of the opening Psalm, but Benedict ordered that the first Psalm at Lauds, the early morning Office, should always be said slowly, so that everyone stood a chance of getting there (Ch. 13 of the *Rule*).

What we do 'as a rule' must not be a burden, but a framework which frees us to grow in love. Rooted in paying attention to God, like the Celts who had a prayer for every occasion, we learn to make the connections, and live every part of our lives to God's praise and glory.

Eucharistic Prayer – St Benedict

Lord God, we praise you
for your servant Benedict,
who turned from earthly wealth
to discover the rich simplicity
of your love:
Lord, teach us to measure our lives
by the fullness of Christ.

We thank you for Benedict's insight
that all relationships should be
governed by humility:
Teach us to respect each other
and all creation.

We thank you for his teaching
that obedience is the
touchstone of faith:
Lord, bring our hearts back
to desire your will.

We thank you for his insistence
that where we are
is where we shall find you:
Lord, open our eyes that we may see.

With Benedict and all whose lives
have been inspired by his Rule,
we join angels and archangels
and the whole company of heaven, saying:
Holy, holy, holy Lord,
God of life and love,
heaven and earth are full of your glory,
all praise to your name.

Be with us, Lord God,
as we remember Jesus,
who on the night before he died,
took bread and wine, gave you thanks,
and gave them to his friends, saying,
'This is my body, this is my blood.
Eat and drink to remember me.'

**Come to us now, Lord God,
and call us afresh to your service.
Keep us faithful, make us joyful,
for you are the God who delights in us
and rejoices to call us your friends. Amen.**

Re-charge or re-tune

People often talk about times of retreat, or periods for more sustained reflection on their Christian life, as *recharging their batteries.* I've been unhappy with that imagery for some time, but only recently have I realized why. Batteries are items that we have to supply ourselves in order to make things work, as we often discover to our irritation when we unpack whatever we've bought, and find that we should have read the small print that tells us that batteries are not supplied. Rechargeable batteries don't work for ever either – sooner or later they lose their capacity for supplying energy.

Our Christian faith, on the other hand, however we have embraced it, whether through Baptism or some other form of commitment, connects us straight to the mains, the source of Life. The love of God, shown to us supremely through the life, death and resurrection of Jesus, embraces us in the life-giving power of the Spirit.

The trouble is that our reception gets distorted through the static of our pre-occupations, and the interference of our busy-ness. So from time to time, we need to *re-tune*, and perhaps clean or sharpen up our contact points.

I find that more helpful imagery, because it reminds us that the initiative always lies with God. What we are called to do is respond – our responsibility lies in making ourselves as open and receptive as we can be to God's gift of life. Retreats, Quiet Days and our regular prayer times are all opportunities to learn that open-ness.

Quiet Day

What is a Quiet Day for? Most of us rush around from one thing to another for much of the time. A Quiet Day offers us space to rest and recover ourselves. Quite often, if we do nothing we suffer from a terrible feeling of guilt, because we've inherited the view that really we ought always to be on the go. Not all the Victorian values were good ones, and the reinforcement of Kipling's idea about 'filling the unforgiving minute with sixty seconds' worth of distance run' (in his poem 'If'), which hymns like 'Father, hear the prayer we offer' put in front of us, encourages a kind of spirituality which leaves no time for resting in God.

My response to that hymn is the poem:

The prayer we offer

Not for ease? Why not?
What's wrong with ease?
For most of us the
Problem is not self-indulgence,
But that we allow ourselves too little.
Prohibitions, counsels of perfection,
Drive us and load us up with guilt.

Time enough for courageous living
And all that rock-smiting.
Let's rest and wander in green pastures
When we find them, make the space
To let ourselves be loved;
Build up our strength
And grow in confidence;
Drink living water springing in
Great fountains;
Feed on the Bread of Life which
Satisfies.

Then we shall have provision
For the journey, and at last
Arrive, not too unpractised
In the art of resting
In his presence.[1]

A Quiet Day gives us just that opportunity for letting ourselves be loved. We don't *have* to do anything – it's not a day for catching up on odd jobs or unwritten letters, or even reading a good book. It's a day for doing nothing with God, letting God slow us down, fill us with his life, and send us back to what we call 'normal' life with fresh courage and a deeper sense of God's presence. If you haven't got time, it's definitely a day for you.

Note

1. *Watching for the Kingfisher*, p. 13.

Planning and leading a Quiet Day

The leader and the organizer of a Quiet Day need to be in touch well in advance, to discuss the form and content of the day, so that the event itself can run smoothly.

Also think about the cost of the day. How much will the venue charge? What expenses will the leader incur? Does the leader expect a fee? It is a good idea to give the leader a token of some kind if there is no fee involved – a lot of work goes into the preparation, and participants should have the opportunity to recognize that.

With regard to the content of the day, consider who the day is for. Will participants be familiar with the use of silence, or new to it? For some, the idea of a day spent in silence sounds very attractive, for others it's rather daunting. For people who live alone, and perhaps meet few people in the course of daily life, to spend time with others but not be able to talk to them might be very hard, even cruel. There are no brownie points awarded for the length of time we spend in silence, but stillness does deepen if we give it a chance, so arrange for definite periods of quiet during the day. The crunch point usually comes at lunch time. Perhaps it would be possible to set aside one area for people who want to be quiet all day, and then people could choose whether to talk or not as they eat. (It is probably a good idea for the leader to join any non-silent group at lunch, so that they don't feel in any way 'second class'.) Usually the simplest way to provide lunch is for people to bring their own. If lunch is being provided, and will be served in one place, negotiate with the group at the beginning of the day, or beforehand, about the place of silence during the day. Whatever the experience of participants, or lack of it, some basic help at the beginning of the day about using the time will be welcomed.

It might be helpful to call the event 'A Day for Quiet Reflection', rather than 'A Quiet Day'. Make it clear in the publicity material what is likely to happen, so that people know what to expect. A basic programme might look like this:

10.00	Arrive, coffee
10.15	Worship, introduction of theme and first address followed by time for personal reflection
12 noon	Corporate prayer or a simple Eucharist
12.30	Lunch
1.30	Address followed by time for personal reflection
2.45	Closing worship
3.00	Tea and depart.

The times can be adjusted, but some people will have children to collect from school, or other commitments in the early evening, so it is best not to end too late.

The content of the day may be requested by the group, or it may be left to the leader to decide. Whatever it is, the leader needs to be clear in his/her own mind about the content of the day. The participants should be given clear indications about timing, and offered a variety of activities (without compulsion!) for the periods of personal reflection. The most important activity is to do nothing, and let God love us, but most of us need a few ideas to explore to help us reach that kind of stillness.

Choose the venue with care, and if possible visit it before you decide to use it. It should be warm (well ventilated in summer) and reasonably comfortable to sit in, with a kitchen so that people can make drinks when they want them, and loos nearby. You do not have to go into the depths of the country – in fact, it's bad theology to think that we can't be still and meet God in the middle of a city. But the content of the day will to some extent be determined by the environment, and perhaps by the weather.

Wherever the day is held, if possible find a space where the corporate parts of the day can be contained, such as a chapel or a circle of chairs. Provide a worship focus – candle, icon, flowers – and perhaps a helpful background aroma. Make sure you can be heard – use a loop system if it exists.

Checklist for the organizer

Do participants know what they need to bring, such as a Bible, and material to write or draw with?

Do they know what the day will cost?

Are people sure about travel arrangements?

Will there be a Eucharist? What will be needed for it?

Checklist for the leader

Do you have everything that you need: copies of any material you want people to ponder over; Bible references; words of hymns/songs; candles?

If you want to sing, can you lead the singing unaccompanied? If you need accompaniment, do you know if anyone can play the flute/violin/guitar? (More suitable for a small group than piano/organ.)

Will you need a tape recorder/CD player? (Don't forget to bring CDs/tapes.) Is there a convenient socket to plug a machine into, or will you need an extension lead?

If there is to be a Eucharist, what do you need to provide?

Remember, people have come to spend time with God. The leader's job is to enable that, not to fill the space. **Be brief.**

Give basic guidance as the day progresses. **Be simple.**

What leaders have to offer springs out of their own prayerfulness. **Be prepared through prayer, and make sure that there is a network of people praying for the day.**

A simple order for a Eucharist

The principle behind this order of service is that there should be few words, and plenty of space for reflection. The whole order is intended to reflect confidence in the love of God who has put away our sin, and welcomes us as his chosen people. Familiar prayers can be used, but sparingly. It is possible to use this outline for an extended Eucharist on the last morning of a retreat, with the last address forming part of the Ministry of the Word, and a break for reflection (and possibly coffee) preceding the Offertory.

Preparation (a simple prayer invoking the Holy Spirit)

Invitation to confession (based on words from Julian of Norwich)

The Lord looks on his servants with pity,
not with blame.
In our sight we do not stand;
in God's sight we do not fall.
Both these insights are true,
but the greater belongs to God.

Confession

Either leave space for silent confession, or use the following form:

Lord God, you have made us for yourself, and long for our love;
forgive our reluctance to respond to you.
Lord, have mercy:
Lord, have mercy.

Lord Christ, you bring us healing and forgiveness;
forgive our unwillingness to accept your gifts.
Christ, have mercy:
Christ, have mercy.

Lord Spirit, you come to us with new life;
forgive our desire to cling on to old ways.
Lord, have mercy:
Lord, have mercy.

Absolution

Our merciful God has put away your (our) sin.
Let us take hold of this forgiveness, and live
in confidence and peace. **Amen.**

Collect

Reading(s)

Silence for reflection

Prayers – the litany for the world, at the end of the section on Praying for the world, section 1 p. 33, would be a useful, simple form of intercession.

Offertory – as well as the traditional prayers at the offering of the bread and wine, it would be appropriate to say:

Blessed are you, Lord God of all creation,
of your goodness we have *our* gifts to offer.
Blessed by your grace, we shall shine as lights in the world.

Eucharistic Prayer

(There are several Eucharistic prayers with the seasonal material in this book.)

The Lord's Prayer

Invitation to share Communion

(It would be good at this point, if not before, if participants were in a circle, so that they could give the bread and wine to each other. If words are required, the *Wee Worship Book*, Fourth Incarnation, from the Iona Community has some suggestions.)

Share Communion

Prayer of thanksgiving

Blessing and Dismissal (Jeu d'Esprit)

Flame-dancing Spirit, come,
Sweep us off our feet and
Dance us through our days.
Surprise us with your rhythms,
Dare us to try new steps, explore
New patterns and new partnerships.
Release us from old routines
To swing in abandoned joy
And fearful adventure.
And in the intervals,
Rest us,
In your still centre.[1]

We go in peace to love and serve the Lord:
In the name of Christ. Amen.

Note

1. *Watching for the Kingfisher*, p. 91.

A day to let God love you

Material for a Quiet Day using the pattern set out in 'Planning and leading a Quiet Day' (section 3 p. 180).

Preparation

It will be helpful to have:

A handout listing Bible references: Genesis 1.26, 31; Isaiah 43.4; Ephesians 2.8–10 (Jerusalem Bible version); Mark 10.17–22 (rich young man); Luke 19.1–10 (Zacchaeus); Matthew 16.13–23, 26.31–46, Luke 22.54–62, John 21.15–17 (Peter); John 15.12–17, and the poem 'Revelation'. This can be given to participants after the first session to help them follow up the material if they want to – there won't be an examination at the end of the day!

Another handout for the afternoon session, containing the extract from Henri Nouwen's *Life of the Beloved*. (Found in the section 'Becoming the Beloved – Taken'.)[1]

A reproduction of Michelangelo's *Captives* is a useful visual aid.

A candle as a centre focus. Individual candles for use in closing worship.

Material for worship, including a map of the world and leaves.

Outline for introductory address

Today you haven't got to do anything but let God love you. We're not very good at doing that. We put a lot of energy into working out how we can love God, but we don't let God have much of a chance to love us. That is partly because we don't think we are very lovable. If God knew what I was really like, he'd never love me – but when we catch ourselves thinking like that, it's time to reassess things.

St Theresa told her nuns to try thinking of God looking at them lovingly and humbly. That's not the way we often think about God looking at us. We carry within us still folk memories of the Victorian all-seeing eye of God, looking at everything we do, and disapproving of most of it.

But that is not the biblical view of God and God's relationship with us. First of all, we are told that we are made in the image of God, (Genesis 1.26) and that when he had made everything, he was delighted with it (Genesis 1.31). Then Paul tells us (in Ephesians 2.10 in the Jerusalem Bible version) that we are God's work of art. Not the description we often give ourselves, perhaps. But if we have ever looked at anything we have made and thought that it's pretty good, then we begin to understand something of what God feels for each one of us. We are precious and honoured, and loved (Isaiah 43.4).

That doesn't mean that we are perfect. We have some way to go still – we are a bit like Michelangelo's *Captives*, still in the process of being completed. But not being complete is the human condition. Even when our flaws are to be laid at our own door, what in church language we call 'sin' is not the most important thing about us. The most important thing is what God sees – our potential, our giftedness, the special qualities each one of us has. It would be wonderful if, each time we met for worship, we could balance the time we spend reflecting on our sinfulness by spending some time reflecting thankfully on our giftedness. That would help us to get our view of ourselves back into God's perspective. We might also be able to think of him more realistically as our Father: most parents talking about their children rejoice in their good points, rather than dwelling on their bad ones. And even when talking about their naughtiness, they find it difficult sometimes to keep their faces straight. I wonder sometimes whether God has the same difficulty with us!

We can learn about the way God looks at us by thinking about the way Jesus looked at people in his encounters.

He looked at the rich young man with love, as he told him to get rid of his riches and then follow him. The young man couldn't do it. But I wonder if, when he reflected on the conversation later, he realized that for the first time someone had told him to give his wealth away because he was wanted for himself, not for what he had got? Did he, perhaps, in the end, decide to follow?

Jesus looked up to Zacchaeus, and told him he wanted to spend time with him. The first time for years, perhaps, that anyone had looked *up* to Zacchaeus, and seen him for who he really was. We know the transformation that resulted from that look.

And Peter – Jesus looked at him in the courtyard, just after Peter had denied knowing him. It must have been a look of love and acceptance to make Peter weep bitterly. And then, after the resurrection, by another charcoal fire, Jesus restored Peter through his threefold question, 'Do you love me?' The language in the Greek is significant. When Jesus asked the question, Peter responded with a rather weaker word for love, 'I am your friend.' The second time the same thing happens. But the third time, Jesus uses Peter's word, 'Are you my friend?' Peter is uncomfortable at the questioning – but Jesus doesn't go on to say that when Peter can love him properly, he will entrust him with his work; he commissions him there and then, and helps Peter move towards wholeness again.

That is most encouraging for us in our discipleship – whatever the level of commitment we can give, Jesus looks at us with love, and takes us as we are, so that he can grow us to wholeness.

So this morning, think about God looking at you with love, appreciating you and your gifts, and rejoice with God in them.

Go on, Lord,
Love me into wholeness,
Set me free
To share with you
In your creative joy;
To laugh with you
At your delight
In me,
Your work of art.[2]

Midday prayer (or Simple Eucharist)

Use the map and leaves as suggested in 'Praying for the world' (in Section 1 p. 32). Being loved by God, and special to him, is not the same as being spoilt, so it is good to spend time praying for all whom God loves, and for whom we feel concern.

Outline for second address

'You are precious in my eyes and honoured, and I love you' (Isaiah 43.4).

What, me? We are so conditioned to backing off from compliments and thanks that we find it very difficult to accept that we are loved. Just think of how we respond when someone gives us an unexpected present. 'Oh, you shouldn't have done that,' we say.

Or 'You shouldn't have spent all that on me'! What does that say about our sense of self-worth?

Jesus says we are special. We have been chosen. But we have had so many experiences of not being chosen that it is hard to believe. It all began probably in the playground when the teams were being picked, and the best friends and the good at games got chosen first. The group of those not picked got smaller and smaller, and there was an awful feeling that I might be the only one left, not really wanted but having to join the team because you had to go somewhere. We can all remember hurts like that. And there may well have been more serious ones, when relationships didn't work out, or a coveted job went to someone else. It's easy to think we're not worth much.

But Jesus says he has chosen us. We often get our discipleship the wrong way round, and think we have chosen him. But his love always draws us before we respond. And his choice is that we become his friends, working with him, bearing fruit as his life flows through us. Henri Nouwen, in *Life of the Beloved* says, 'The great spiritual battle begins – and never ends – with the reclaiming of our chosen-ness.' We have to allow God to look at us and say, 'You are precious, I have chosen you, and love you', and not draw back.

We can all think of reasons why we can't be special and chosen. But we have to challenge those thoughts whenever they come up within us, or attack us from outside, and assert again that we have been chosen by God for himself. But we are not more special than God's other people. When we really begin to learn about love, we learn that the more we give away, the more we have. Becoming confident in our own sense of being loved will enable us to help others to be aware that they are loved too.

And perhaps we shall be able to challenge the heresy that we always have to be on the go to earn God's favour. Let's look at our diaries, and see whether we could plan to have time to let God love us every day.

That's something we could try to do this afternoon, as we think about the fact that we have been chosen, and ask for grace to let that truth sink deep into our hearts.

Closing worship

Spend time in thanksgiving for the day.

Give participants the opportunity to light an individual candle as an act of commitment to live as people chosen and loved. These can be placed on the map, since it is in the world that we live out our calling.

Encourage people to take a candle with them as they leave. The Quiet Day will be over, but what has begun in it will continue as life goes on.

Notes

1. Henri Nouwen, *Life of the Beloved*, Hodder & Stoughton, 1993.
2. 'Revelation', in *Watching for the Kingfisher*, p. 125.

A day with Julian of Norwich
Material for a Quiet Day

This material uses some of the ideas set out in 'A day to let God love you', but takes the illustrations from *The Revelation of Divine Love* by Julian of Norwich.

Preparation

It will be helpful to have:

Handouts containing extracts from chapters 4, 46, 48, 52, 58, 59, 62 of the Long Text of *The Revelation of Divine Love*, and Bible references for maternal imagery for God: Deuteronomy 32.11–12, 18; 33.27; Isaiah 49.15; Hosea 11.1–4; Matthew 23.37, together with Anselm's Canticle beginning 'Jesus, as a mother you gather your people to you,' for follow-up to the first session, and from chapters 39, 40, 73 and 82 of the Long Text for the second session.

For midday worship, use the map of the world and hazelnuts.

At closing worship, individual candles.

Outline for first address

'Everything has being through the love of God.' 'All will be well.'

Julian's message was nothing like the facile message given by some Christians: 'God's in his heaven, all's right with the world.'

Julian knew from her experience that all was not right with the world. Give a brief summary of the current situation in Church and state during her lifetime: The Hundred Years' War began and continued; there were outbreaks of plague;

political unrest leading to the Peasants' Revolt; cattle plague and poor harvests.

Julian's conviction that all will be well came out of her experience when she was just over 30, when she was seriously ill, and was granted a series of visions of Christ, accompanied by revelations of the depth of God's love. From them she drew understanding of the nature of God, and the nature of humanity.

First of all, God.

What is your preferred imagery for God? By what name do you address God? We have got very used to particular ways of addressing or describing God. 'Father' is the most usual and, in hymns, 'King', 'Judge' and 'Shepherd' probably come next in popularity. But we've got stuck, probably because we take Jesus seriously when he said, 'When you pray, say "Our Father".' But when he said that, I wonder whether he wasn't simply suggesting another idea to play with – Father is not a prominent image in the Jewish scriptures.

There is much maternal imagery in Scripture, and when Julian suggested that we might think of God as Mother, she was not the first theologian to do so. Anselm of Canterbury in the tenth century had done so too. Julian attributes to our Mother God our creation, our care in mercy and pity, our sustenance not with milk but with the precious food of true life in the Sacrament. Just as a mother does not want her children to suffer, even to the point of giving her life for them, so God in Jesus our Mother brings us by his death to eternal life.

It isn't necessarily more helpful to address God as Mother than it is to address God as Father – both titles can raise difficulties for people because of their own experiences. But it does widen our understanding to consider the imagery we use. Part of our difficulty lies in the way the English language attaches gender to nouns and pronouns – in many languages that isn't the case, and God has to be God. It is worth noting that imagery is a gift to play with, not a straitjacket to pin God down. We don't turn God into anything by the imagery we use – God doesn't become a rock just because the Psalmist described God in that way. But we are perhaps in danger of turning our idea of God into an idol if we are unwilling to countenance fresh imagery.

So this morning, ponder on imagery. Experiment a little with ideas that may be fresh to you, but are actually very old. You might like to look at the biblical passages referred to. But all our thinking needs to send us back to God, for as Julian said, 'Only in God we have all.'

Midday prayer (or simple Eucharist)

Use map and hazelnuts. (See Praying for the world, Section 1 p. 32.)

Outline for second address

Where does what we were thinking about this morning leave us? How does our imagery for God help us to understand ourselves, and our relationship with God? The way people talk, you would think that God is out to get us. Insurance companies describe as acts of God anything they regard as too nasty to be recognized as qualifying for compensation, never anything good! And we persist in asking what we have done to deserve the things which happen to us, as though God sends suffering and hardship to punish us, even when we don't deserve it. What loving father/mother would act like that?

We have to recognize the fact of sin. But Julian had some very liberating things to say about sin. It is nothing, not because it doesn't exist – it is the sharpest scourge that can afflict us. It is nothing, because it has no status; God has dealt with it, and sin is forgiven. For Julian, feelings of guilt and worthlessness are far more damaging than the failures we call sin, because they fix our attention on ourselves. What really delights God is our delight in him, and preoccupation with sin distracts us from that.

'Our courteous Lord does not want his servants to despair because they fall often and grievously, for our falling does not hinder him in loving us. In our sight we do not stand, in God's sight we do not fall.' Both these insights are true, but the greater belongs to God.

To God, we are infinitely precious and loved, and grasping that truth will help us build up our confidence, and sense of self-worth. For we are chosen. We can all think of reasons why we are not worth choosing, but those are lies. The truth is that we are chosen by God, and God wants us to value ourselves. That doesn't mean that we don't need to change – confession and forgiveness are still necessary. But forgiveness sets us free to move on and grow in confidence in God's love.

There will be several outcomes to this sense of growing self-worth. We will have the grace to stop putting ourselves down by describing ourselves as unworthy recipients of God's love. We might be able to accept gifts and compliments without responding with 'Oh, you shouldn't have done that!' We shall learn that what is true of us is true of everyone else too, and that will affect the way we treat others, and the range of our prayerful support. We shall grow in understanding that we are chosen not so that we can feel smug about it, but because we are meant to bear fruit. That entails pruning, having the dead wood in our lives cut out, letting God train us in the way we need to grow.

We are God's work of art – not finished, but on-the-way people. So this afternoon, ponder on your chosen-ness, and think about how life could be different if we really dared to believe that we are precious to God.

Closing worship

Spend time in thanksgiving for the day.

Give participants the opportunity to light an individual candle as an act of commitment to live as people chosen and loved. These can be placed on the map, since it is in the world that we live out our calling.

Encourage people to take a candle with them as they leave. The Quiet Day will be over, but what has begun in it will continue as life goes on.

Eucharistic Prayer – Julian of Norwich

Lord God,
through your servant Julian
you revealed to us that
as Father you are all power and goodness,
and as Mother you are all wisdom and love:
We praise and glorify you.

We praise you that you hold
all creation in your love,
and enfold all creatures in your care:
We praise and glorify you.

With angels and archangels
and the whole company of heaven
we sing:
Holy, holy, holy Lord,
God of life and love,
Heaven and earth are full of your glory,
all praise to your name.

Come to us now, Lord God,
as we remember Jesus, who,
on the night before he died,
took bread and wine, blessed them
and gave them to his friends, saying,
'This is my body, this is my blood.
Eat and drink to remember me.'

Come to us now, most courteous God,
and fill our hearts with longing for you:
God of your goodness, give us yourself.

Take from us all hesitancy and fear:
God of your goodness, give us yourself.
Draw us to delight in you, for you are the God who longs for our love:
God of your goodness, give us yourself,
for we can ask for nothing less
than that which can do you full worship.
If we ask anything less,
we shall always be in want.
Only in you we have all. Amen.

A day for carers

A day for carers provides much-needed respite for people who often have little time for themselves, and the programme needs above all to provide space, without much formal input from the leader, who for this purpose could well be renamed the host. Carers often get so overwhelmed by the demands of care that they push their own needs aside, and it is good to offer people a little pampering when they do find time to get away. It is important to have a venue which is comfortable.

I have been blessed in being able to use a local retreat house where we hold two such days most years. Old Alresford Place, in Hampshire, is set in lovely grounds. In the winter we can have a log fire in the sitting-room, and those who come always appreciate the way the table is laid for lunch, and the care with which the food is presented. I have found it helpful to work, on alternate days, alongside an aromatherapist who offers hand massage, and a podiatrist who offers foot massage. We have a general rule that, for the morning at least, we don't talk to the other carers about what we do, so that everyone has a chance to get away from the demands. This is not a day for the exchange of information – other bodies provide days of that kind. While the aromatherapist/podiatrist are plying their skill, I make myself available for personal conversation with anyone who wants to come. I was a carer for nine years myself as my mother became increasingly infirm and senile, and for the last 15 months of her life she was in a home, so I understand something of what people are going through. At lunch we talk, and in the afternoon people either go on with their own pursuits, or enjoy each other's company on a walk, or sitting in the garden or by the fire.

A pattern for the day

Provide coffee as people arrive

(It may not be possible for everyone to arrive for the formal beginning, so make sure there is always someone on hand to make people feel welcome when they do arrive.) If possible, make sure that people can make drinks as and when they want to.

Gathering to set the scene

Light a candle as a reminder for us that Jesus, the light of the world, is with us, and that we are being prayed for.

Play some music to help people 'arrive' and begin to unwind.

Introductory talk

You are special not because you are carers, but because you are the people you are, and God loves you (Isaiah 43.4). We don't always feel that we are special – people tell us sometimes that we are wonderful because of what we do, but we know that caring sometimes brings out the worst in us, and we can feel very guilty about the resentment and irritation that can make us less than kind or even positively murderous. Sometimes we feel guilt about the decisions we have to make about involving professional care in a home. I was greatly helped in this by a comment made to a friend of mine about the situation she was in, long before it became an issue for me. She was told, 'Your mother needs two things, love and care. At the moment, the demands made on you by her care are so great that it is difficult for you to love her. If you can arrange for your mother to be cared for, you will be free to love her.' We don't have to beat ourselves up about having negative feelings – but we need to develop some strategies for making sure that those we care for don't get the rough end of our temper. Time away, like today, is one way of restoring our balance.

Today, you haven't got to do anything. It's time for you. As a physical reminder that you have left your duties behind, write your name on the card, and the name of the person/situation you are having time away from, and put it in the bowl/on the altar, next to the candle which reminds us that we are all in God's hands. We can safely leave our care to him and the people who are standing in for us today. At the end of the day, you can pick the card up again, as you pick up your duties.

I'm going to suggest that we give each other space to get away from the demands – so let's agree that we won't talk to each other about what we have to do as carers, at least for this morning. If you want to talk about your situation, I'm here for you – I know from personal experience what it's like. There is a sheet of paper where you can book your time for personal pampering with hand/foot massage, and you can book a slot with me too if you want. But you don't *have* to do anything! You can walk, sleep, have a long undisturbed bath . . . take your time.

During the day

Sometimes I suggest that we have a time of prayer together before lunch.

Sometimes we have a formal ending, largely a time of thanksgiving, and prayer for encouragement as we continue the care.

People are not always able to stay for the whole day, so the host needs to be around as much as possible to make them feel at home while they are there.

Material for use in a Quiet Garden

People who open their gardens for The Quiet Garden Movement sometimes like to offer a theme for the day. These days do not usually have a formal programme following the introductory meditation. If there is a Eucharist, the prayer which follows these suggested themes might be considered to be appropriate.

Theme 1: Consider the flowers

The kiss of the sun for pardon
The song of the birds for mirth
One is nearer God's heart in a garden
Than anywhere else on earth.

'God's Garden', Dorothy Frances Gurney

That isn't true, and it's bad theology. What is true is that we often *feel* closer to God. There is peace and refreshment in being alongside the growing life of a garden or the countryside, which often contrasts with the busyness of ordinary life. But that is a city-dweller's view – country people know that there is a lot of hard work behind the tranquillity. And, actually, any gardener knows that there is conflict and a struggle to survive within all growth. And there are always the slugs – a great theological challenge to town- and country-dwellers alike.

But what might we learn from the flowers as we consider them today?

First, each has its own beauty. Take a long look at the flowers, and appreciate their variety in colour and shape, the texture and shade of their greenery.

They all contribute something to the beauty of the whole, partly by enhancing the beauty of other plants.

Don't ignore the plants that don't seem to be doing very

much. Some contribute their sober foliage as a background against which others stand out. There are some exotic beauties which seem to stand out on their own, but even they are often glad of a bit of support, especially when the wind and the rain batter them about.

We might go on to think about ourselves. What are our strengths and beauty? What do we contribute to the human herbaceous border which is so dear to God's heart? Some of our gifts may not seem too obvious: like some plants we might look rather dull, or be rather prickly. But it is just those which provide support for the plants around them. So let's acknowledge our nature, and give thanks for who we are, and ask God's blessing on our flowering.

Then we might ponder on the life of plants, and remember that there is always change and growth. If a seed doesn't break open, there will be no plant. If the plant does not flower there will be no chance for it to bear its fruit, which contains the seed for the next generation. The end of all growth is fruitfulness.

In my garden, the prickly firethorn which keeps me at arm's length is covered with berries which will feed the birds, and there is a profusion of love-in-the-mist seed heads which are more beautiful than the flowers. So we might think about ourselves, about our own progress towards fruitfulness. That won't mean for all of us ensuring that there is a new generation to keep the human race going. Our fruitfulness may be in the wisdom we can bring in maturity to our dealings with others, and the way we order our own lives.

And we might remember again how important it is to move on – clinging to the stage where we feel most beautiful or useful, or regretting its passing, means that we prevent ourselves from recognizing the beauty of the present. Some people, like some plants, really come into their own in old age.

The rhythm of nature is sustained by God's love. Our world *is*, our life *is*, because God loves us and wants to bring us to fruitfulness and maturity. And death is part of that process – we carry the seed of eternity within us, which in God's time will be set free.

Theme 2: Trees

The Jewish/Christian story begins in a garden where there were plenty of trees. Only two of them are named: the tree of knowledge, and the tree of life (Genesis 2.9).

We have spent so much of our time in Christian history weighed down by guilt at having tasted the fruit of the forbidden tree, that we seem to have forgotten that God didn't tell anyone not to eat fruit from the tree of life.

Today gives us the opportunity to spend time thinking about that tree, and our lives, as we enjoy the presence of trees in this garden.

One of the images of fulfilment in the Old Testament is a tree. Planted by the waterside, or rooted in worship, trees flourish and bear fruit (Psalm 1.1–3; Jeremiah 17.7–8; Psalm 92.12–15). Jesus used tree imagery too, when he said, 'I am the vine, you are the branches' (John 15.5). Notice that he didn't say, 'I am the *stem*, you are the branches', but 'I am the *vine*'. He enfolds us in his life: we draw his life into ourselves in order to bear fruit. We are inextricably part of him, and he of us. As Paul wrote in Galatians 2.20, 'It is no longer I who live, but it is Christ who lives in me.' Paul used tree imagery also when he wrote in his letter to the Ephesians that it was his prayer for them 'that Christ may dwell in your hearts through faith, as you are being rooted and grounded in love' (Ephesians 3.17). Right at the end of the Bible, the tree of life appears again, and its leaves are for the healing of the nations (Revelation 22.2).

We bring all that to our enjoyment of trees today. And we can add some observations of our own too.

Trees are welcoming – they give life and shelter to myriads of creatures. We enjoy their shelter and shade, and use them as meeting places, trysting places.

They provide stability – we see what happens when rain forests are destroyed, and whole ecological systems are wiped out.

They offer us, as all plants do, a pattern of life that includes death. They can't cling on to any stage of their development: flowers and fruit have to die before new life can be released.

Their roots are amazing: they push through all kinds of debris and unyielding materials in search of life.

So we have plenty of food for thought as we enjoy the trees around us. Let's look and touch, enjoy the texture of the bark, think about the roots, stretch up with the branches. And then let's use our imagination about our own lives. Where are our roots? Can we claim the negative, unyielding bits of our own experience and draw nourishment from them as well as from the more pleasurable springs of life?

And our branches. Do we need to prune our lifestyle so that energy is used more efficiently and fruitfully? Are we welcoming, offering healing in relationships and chance encounters?

But most of all, let's relax into the quiet rhythm of the trees' lives, and feel the sap rising in us again.

Peace Trees

To be in the presence of trees
Is to know peace.
The silent rhythm of their life,
Bringing maturity in due time,
Without anxiety or haste,
Calms our impatience;
Their solid strength, derived from
Hidden roots spreading much further
Than we ever know, gives us security;
Grace, beauty, shapeliness and form,
Delight our senses, soothe our
Fragile nerves, and bring refreshment.

Let us in turn be trees,
Growing in God's time to maturity,
Spreading our roots deep into springs of life,
Opening branches wide to all who come,
Offering strength and healing through our
Peace.[1]

Theme 3: Consider the birds

(This section takes its name from the title of the poem.)

That's one command
I have no problem with.

I held a swallow once,
Knocked senseless by some accident;
Fragile body, tiny beating heart
Cupped in my hand. Then, restored,
With flirt of feathers
Off to freedom flight.

I who have scarcely
Stirred beyond these shores,
Held one who, twice at least,
Had flown four thousand miles.
No map, no compass,
Only unerring inner certainty
Carrying him over land and ocean.
A moment to treasure.

Then there are sparrows,
So common we don't notice them;
Eight a penny, or perhaps ten
Since decimalization.
I wonder why you didn't tell Job
To look at sparrows, instead of
Parading the juggernauts of your

Creation. After all,
Anyone could make a hippopotamus –
No finesse there, a lump with
Four legs and a great big head –
A child's production.
But a sparrow, there's craftsmanship:
Those shades of brown and gold,
Arranged and sculpted into
Subtly beautiful plumage,
Each one different;
The stocky bodies full of energy,
Brisk, going about their business,
Fighting, squabbling,
Caring for their young, chirping
In incessant cheerfulness.

In contrast to the heron,
Standing more still than a
Contemplative, alert
Waiting for the moment.

And no-one could watch ducks,
Or, better still, listen to them,
Without believing in your sense of humour.

Kingfisher's glory, blackbird's song,
The miracle of flight itself . . .
The list is endless.

And we more precious.
A mystery to ponder.[2]

For years now I've been a birdwatcher. Not a twitcher – twitchers rush off whenever something rare or unusual is reported, so that they can say they've seen it, and tick it off on their list. But they don't necessarily learn much about the bird in question, which is often out of context, away from its normal habitat, blown off-course by a storm.

Watchers, on the other hand, wait, look, consider, take time to be where the birds are: a much more contemplative way. They go out in all weathers, sometimes see very little, and from time to time, have one of those rewarding moments which make it all worthwhile.

All that has its parallels in our spiritual life. We sometimes rush off to get the latest spiritual experience, an instant glow of holiness, or a spiritual high. We could learn from the bird *watchers* to be still, alert, but not anxious, eyes open and aware. Ready to receive what we are given.

Bird watching has taught me that all is gift. I may go out hoping to see a particular bird – but it may not be in evidence. I can't control the movement of the birds. And if I am too intent on seeing one particular bird, I may miss a lot of other things that are around. Prayer is like that:

Disclosure

Prayer is like watching for the
Kingfisher. All you can do is
Be where he is likely to appear, and
Wait.
Often, nothing much happens;
There is space, silence and
Expectancy.
No visible sign, only the
Knowledge that he's been there,
And may come again.
Seeing or not seeing cease to matter,
You have been prepared.
But sometimes, when you've almost
Stopped expecting it,
A flash of brightness
Gives encouragement.[3]

So it's all gift. The work we have to do is be prepared, in the right habitat, with the right disposition. And then we have to respond, with thanksgiving for God's amazing love which cares even for the sparrows, endangered species that they are.

Kingfisher's glory, blackbird's song, the mystery of migration, the miracle of flight. And we are more precious. A mystery to ponder.

Surrounded by birds, where better to spend the day pondering?

Notes

1. *Watching for the Kingfisher*, p. 23.
2. Ibid., p. 26.
3. Ibid., p. 31.

A creation Eucharist

Preparation

Lord God, you created all that is;
We praise you and bless you.
You honoured humanity with the image of your likeness;
We praise and bless you.
You entrusted us with the wellbeing of all you have made;
We praise and bless you, living God.

But we have failed to live up to your desire that we should reflect your image, and we come in penitence to ask forgiveness.

Lord God, you created the world, and it was very good. Forgive us when we mis-use your creation and exploit your creatures.
Lord, have mercy. **Lord, have mercy.**

Lord Christ, you long to gather us to you, as a hen gathers her chicks to protect them. Forgive us when we turn away.
Christ have mercy. **Christ, have mercy.**

Holy Spirit, as at the beginning of creation, you bring life to all created beings. Forgive us when we refuse to accept it.
Lord , have mercy. **Lord, have mercy.**

May God forgive us
and set us free to love and serve him
with the whole of our being,
through Jesus Christ our Lord, **Amen.**

Collect

Lord God,
you made us to reflect your glory;
perfect your image in us,
that we may live to your praise,
and share your love with all around us.
For the sake of Jesus Christ, our Lord. **Amen.**

Readings: Psalm 84.1–4
Matthew 6.25–26; 10.29–31

Address

Prayers

Eucharistic prayer

Lord God of all creation,
among all the wonderful things you have made,
we praise you especially for the beauty of birds.
We thank you for their song; for the miracle of flight,
for their tenacity in holding on to life,
for the pleasure they give to all who watch them.
Taught by your Son, we consider them, and with them
we join the angels and archangels to praise you, saying

Holy, holy, holy Lord,
God of love and light.
Heaven and earth and all creation
are full of your glory.

Be with us now, creator God, as we remember Jesus,
Who, on the night before he died, took bread and wine,
Blessed them and gave them to his friends, saying,
'This is my body, given for you,
This is my blood, shed for you;
Eat and drink to remember me.'

Come freshly to us now, Lord God,
and let these gifts of bread and wine
fill us with your life.
As the swallow and the sparrow
find a home in your house,
so may we always be at home in your presence;
as the birds are fed and cared for by your bounty,
So may we rest assured in your constant care.

Keep us alert and expectant, ready to receive you,
and may the music of our worship
join with the song of the birds to your eternal praise:
Blessing and honour and glory are yours,
Lord God of all creation. Amen.

The Lord's prayer

We share Communion

Prayer of thanksgiving

O what a gift, what a wonderful gift!
What have we done to deserve it?
Nothing, absolutely nothing.
No wonder our hearts dance.

Father of all, we give you thanks and praise, that
you have fed us with your life,
and sustain us with your love.
May we who have received your gifts
share your life with others;
may we respect your creation
and live in harmony with all,
for the sake of Jesus Christ, our Lord. Amen.

Blessing

May God surprise us into new recognition of his presence, new understanding of his will, and deep assurance of his love.
And the blessing . . . . . .

We go in peace to love and serve the Lord
In the name of Christ, Amen.

We offer each other a sign of peace

Eucharistic Prayer for a Quiet Garden event

(The words at the Sanctus and at the end of the prayer are taken from the hymn, Holy, Holy, Holy is the Lord.)

Creator God,
in whose garden our story began;
we praise and bless you for your continued
nurture and care as we grow in your kingdom.
We thank you for Jesus, who through his life,
death and resurrection opened the way
to fullness of life.
With angels and archangels, and all
who share in your life-giving love, we praise you,
singing:
Holy, holy, holy is the Lord,
holy is the Lord God almighty. *(Repeat)*
Who was, and is, and is to come.
Holy, holy, holy is the Lord.

Come to us now, holy God,
as we remember Jesus,
who on the night before he died
took bread and wine, blessed them
and gave them to his friends, saying,
'Eat and drink to remember me.'

Come freshly to us now, Lord God,
and bless these gifts of bread and wine.
As we receive them, may we be
rooted and grounded more deeply
in your love.
Nourish us with your life-giving Spirit,
and bring us at last to our full flowering,
where we shall glorify you for ever:

Glory, glory, glory to the Lord,
Glory to the Lord God almighty. *(Repeat)*
Who was, and is, and is to come.
Glory, glory, glory to the Lord.

Eucharistic Prayer – St Francis

Father,
We praise you for your servant Francis,
who, bearing in his body the marks of Jesus,
learned to possess everything
without clinging to possessions;
and by embracing the leper
taught us that what is not lovely in us
is loved and healed by your grace.

Rejoicing like him in your great love
in creation, we join all your creatures
in heaven and earth, to praise you, singing
Holy, holy, holy Lord,
God of joy and life;
Heaven and earth are full of your glory,
Hosanna in the highest.

Hear us now as we meet to remember Jesus,
who on the night before he died
took bread and wine,
blessed them, and gave them to his friends
saying, This is my body, this is my blood,
given for you.

Come freshly to us now, Lord God,
and fill us with your Spirit;
that we may be surprised into
new discoveries of the simplicity
and generosity of your love,
through Jesus Christ our Lord, **Amen.**

Meditation for a flower festival

Jesus said, 'Consider . . .'
Look steadily at the heart of what you contemplate;
be still, and know.

So we consider the flowers, their fragrance, their beauty, their perfection in simplicity.
We consider the flowers, and we give thanks to God for his great glory.

Let us bless the Lord:
Thanks be to God.

We consider the patience and tenacity of flowers – the years through which seeds lie dormant, until the time is right, the opportunity comes; perhaps through natural progression, perhaps through sudden upheaval, as when a motorway scars its way through the countryside, and the verges blaze with blood-red poppies.

We consider the flowers, and we give thanks to God for his patient love.

Let us bless the Lord:
Thanks be to God.

We consider the brokenness of flowers, through which new life comes. Unless the flower blooms and dies, it cannot produce seed; unless a seed dies, it cannot live, but when it falls to the ground and is broken open, new life begins.

We consider the flowers, and we give thanks to God for the life that he gives, through many deaths and resurrections making us whole.

Let us bless the Lord:
Thanks be to God.

We consider the flowers, and give thanks for the artistry and skill and hard work of those who have given us pleasure through this festival.

We consider the flowers, and we give thanks for all God's goodness.

Let us bless the Lord:
Thanks be to God.

We consider the flowers, and our own flowering: the pain and struggle with which our own creativity, in skills and relationships, gives birth and comes to fruition.

We consider the flowers, and we give thanks to God that places of darkness and pain as well as those of joy and light are places where his Spirit works.

Let us bless the Lord:
Thanks be to God.

We consider the flowers, and we give thanks for the way their shapes and colours and fragrances complement each other.

We consider the flowers, and we give thanks for the flowering of life in our community.

Let us bless the Lord:
Thanks be to God.

Planning a walk or a mini-pilgrimage

All over the world, through the centuries, people have gone on pilgrimage to holy places, for all sorts of reasons. A pilgrimage is about walking in someone else's footsteps, making someone else's story your own, asking about the significance of a place in God's eyes, becoming aware. It is often a journey made in the company of others, sharing memories and observations, a serious enterprise, and also fun.

You don't have to go to Mecca, or Jerusalem, or Canterbury. Our own localities have places of significance and people to remember too. All you need for a pilgrimage is some local knowledge, a bit of imagination, and, if possible, a few people to join you.

You don't need to draw attention to yourselves: a pilgrimage is not like a procession of witness, though other people may well be rather curious, and tag along.

You may want to use the walk to increase awareness of the goodness of God in creation. If that is the case, instead of remembering events of significance in the past, you could use the Benedicite (found in Morning Prayer in Anglican Prayer Books) as the basis for reflection.

Whatever the purpose, do the walk yourself first, and decide on the 'stations' – places to pause – and what you will do at each one. A useful pattern is:

- Stop and look.
- Listen to a reflection either about what you see now, or the significance of the place in the past.
- Pause for personal reflection.
- Pray together about the material you have been considering.
- Use a pilgrimage prayer which all can say – something like, 'Lord, keep us faithful and hopeful, and enable us to show your love in the world.'

- Walk on. It is not necessary to be silent on the walk – part of the value of a pilgrimage is that people become more aware of each other as well as God. Be ready for participants to make their own observations, too; you may well have a local historian or a naturalist in the group, and their contribution can add a great deal to the event.

Don't try to do too much – two and a half hours may be quite enough to tackle in a morning or an afternoon. Lunch could be part of the event, in which case try to arrange for a suitable place to have it, either provided by someone not on the walk, or a picnic. End with a 'cuppa' – it is important to share food and drink on these occasions.

You may wish to end in a church or hall or someone's home, and spend a few minutes reflecting on the experience, noting where and how God was present to you.

Make it clear in the publicity what kind of event it will be, and arrange an alternative activity in case of rain. It would be possible to set the 'stations' in a church if the weather is inclement. Simon Bailey's book, *Stations*,[1] has some imaginative ideas for a pilgrimage round your church, town, home or body, depending on your degree of mobility. No one need be excluded, but you do need to be realistic about what people can manage physically.

Note

1. Simon Bailey, *Stations*, Cairns Publications, 1991.

Eucharistic Prayer for city dwellers

Lord of all life,
whose disciples were told
to wait in the city
until they were empowered by your Spirit;
we thank you for our calling to be in this city,
to recognize and name your power
in obvious and unlikely places.
With people on many different paths of faith
who seek the common good, we praise you, saying:
Holy and life-giving God,
vulnerable and strong,
all you have made is full of your glory,
all praise to your name.

Come freshly to us, living God.
Free us from the fear that the task
will be too great;
encourage us with signs of your presence,
and nourish us with the life of your Son,
who, on the night before he died,
took bread and wine, blessed them
and gave them to his disciples, saying,
'This is my body given for you.
This is my blood shed for you.
Do this to remember me.'

Come then, Lord,
and make yourself known in our streets,
that our city may dance with your life,
and its heart beat with
the power of your love. **Amen.**

Give us this day – Lammas Day

August begins with Lammas Day, Loaf Mass Day, the day in the Book of Common Prayer calendar when a loaf baked with flour from newly harvested corn would be brought into church and blessed. It's one of the oldest points of contact between the agricultural world and the Church. The others were Plough Sunday in early January, the Sunday after Epiphany and the day before work would begin again in the fields after the Christmas festivities, when the ploughs would be brought to church to be blessed; and Rogation days in May, the days before Ascension Day, when God's blessing would be sought on the growing crops. Farming communities have always celebrated the successful gathering in of harvest, but our church observance of Harvest Festival was only introduced in the nineteenth century. Perhaps Lammas Day served that purpose in earlier generations.

One of the things I decided to do when I retired was to learn to make bread. I'd made several attempts over the years which had produced something edible (because the ingredients were edible) but nothing I would have offered to share with others. But with the help of a friend who showed me what to do, I had another go. And I became fascinated by the process. Modern bread-making machines turn out a decent loaf, but there is nothing quite like the hands-on experience.

One of the fascinating things about it is the yeast: that unprepossessing lump of putty-like substance, or even more unlikely looking granules of dried yeast. Give yeast warmth and sugar and liquid, and miraculously it grows before your eyes. And then it makes the dough rise and double its size. It seems irrepressible. Knock the dough down, and leave it to its own devices, and it will double its size again.

In the Middle Ages, one of the names for yeast was 'goddisgoode' – written as one word as though it were God's e-mail address – because, people said, 'it cometh of the grete grece [*sic*] of God'. No one understood its chemistry, or knew its origin, it was a gift from God. Like manna of Old Testament times, pure gift. God is good. That is what lies at the heart of bread.

When Jesus said that he is the Bread of Life, embodied for us now in the Eucharist, he was offering himself as a gift as fundamental to meeting our inner needs as bread is to meeting our physical needs. Through feeding on him, God gives us himself, and that is all we need.

But that isn't the end of it. Jesus used yeast as one of his illustrations about the way the kingdom of God works. And when he gave himself as bread, he said it was for the life of the world (John 6.51). We share God's life so that we can *be* the truth that God is good.

God is good. World events and the circumstances of our lives will often knock that truth about, knock it down as dough is knocked down. But God's goodness is irrepressible, and the warmth of our response will help people to recognize it. That's the heart of evangelism: to help people to know the goodness of God. People outside the Church, and some within it, too, judging by some of the debates we've been having recently, seem to think that the Christian life is all about having a set of rules to live by – not a very life-enhancing approach. Jesus offers us something more deeply satisfying, the Bread of Life which assures us that God is good, and meets our deepest needs.

Christians are not people who occupy the high moral ground, who have got the answers to all life's problems. As the Indian evangelist D.T. Niles has said, 'Evangelism is witness. It is one beggar telling another beggar where to get food.'[1] The task of evangelism is to share the good news of God's goodness, and invite others to enjoy the Bread of Life too.

Note

1 D. T. Niles, *That They May Have Life*, Lutterworth, 1952, p. 96.

Prayers at a wedding

Loving God,
we give thanks with N and N
for all the people who have loved and cared for them,
challenged and encouraged them
in their lives so far.
We pray that you will give them the grace
that they need,
as they shape their lives together in marriage:
may they give each other space,
and support each other with sensitivity;
may they meet difficulties with courage and humour,
and enjoy the good times with thankfulness;
may their friendships and their hospitality
spring always from deep commitment to each other
and to you;
and may they continue to grow
in knowledge and experience of
the riches of your love.
We ask this in the name of Christ. **Amen.**

Gracious God,
you call us all to be channels of your grace;
may we who are witnesses to this marriage
support N and N in their life together:
may we set them free from old expectations
to live their life in increasing joy;
may we be ready to listen,
and generous in our understanding;
give us wisdom to know when to speak
and when to be silent;
may N and N find in us
resources of friendship
appropriate to their need.

Come freshly to us all, Lord God:
keep us faithful to your call,
that in all our relationships
we may be signs
of your kingdom of peace and love;
and so we pray:
Our Father . . .

Suggestion for an introduction to a marriage service after a divorce

With the bride and groom standing at the front of the church, facing each other, but apart, the minister addresses the congregation:

Minister: N and N have come to celebrate their marriage, (each) with memories of a previous relationship. They want, as they prepare to make their vows to each other, to give thanks for all that was good in those partnerships (*especially their children), to acknowledge responsibility for their own part in the breakdown of their first marriage, and to ask forgiveness for their own personal failures to live in love.

Minister, addressing N and N:

N and N, you have talked with each other, and faced as honestly as you can the reasons for the breakdown of your previous relationships. Each of you is loved by God, and nothing you have done has put you beyond that love. You, like all of us, need assurance that God's love is greater than our failures, and I invite you now to open yourselves again to the healing power of God's forgiveness.**

Silence

We say together:

**Compassionate God,
come to us and heal us;
forgive our failures to love,
and free us from guilt
about what is past.
Help us to love and serve you
wholeheartedly
in our new relationship
with each other.**

Minister: God in his mercy sets us free.
Take hold of this forgiveness
and live your lives together
in joy and freedom in God's love. **Amen.**

* omit if there are no children

** At this point the minister could add something along these lines:

N and N have identified their particular need, but we all stand in need of forgiveness, and all of us can join in these words, whether aloud or in our hearts, and receive God's forgiveness.

Prayers for the blessing of a house

As participants walk round the house, it would be appropriate to sing the Taizé chant 'Ubi Caritas'. Candles may be lit at each 'station'.

At the front door

Lord God, in Jesus Christ, you came and shared the life of an ordinary home. May this house always be a place of welcome. Bless all who come here, and all who receive them, that they may enter in love, and go out with joy. **Amen.**

In the kitchen

Lord, you are the bread of life. May all who prepare food and offer hospitality here know your presence and be sustained by your peace. **Amen.**

In the dining room

Lord, you make yourself known in the breaking of bread. May all who share fellowship at this table be filled with your life. **Amen.**

In the study

Lord, you have the words of life. May all who read and think and join in conversation here be filled with your wisdom, and be led to your truth. **Amen.**

In a quiet room

In quietness and confidence is our strength. May all who come to this room find your peace and encouragement. **Amen.**

In the sitting room

Where two or three are gathered together in your name, Lord, you are there. May all who use this room be assured of your presence. **Amen.**

On the stairs

Lord, you invited your disciples to come apart from the busy demands of life. May we be refreshed and cleansed, and enjoy your gift of sleep. **Amen.**

In the garden

Lord God, you walked in the garden in the cool of the day, and in a garden your Son was first known to be risen from the dead. May this garden be a place of peace and refreshment for all who work and relax in it. **Amen.**

Eucharistic Prayer for a house blessing

Lord God,
we praise you for calling us
to be the household of faith;
and for blessing us with
companions to encourage us
in our loving;
we praise you for giving us gifts
sufficient for our needs,
and in generous measure
to share with our neighbours.
With angels and archangels
and all who through the ages
have responded to your call,
we rejoice and sing:
Holy, holy, holy Lord,
God of life and joy,
Heaven and earth are full of your glory,
Hosanna in the highest.

Come now, Lord, and make your dwelling
in our hearts and homes,
as we remember Jesus, who
on the night before his death,
took bread and wine, blessed them
and gave them to his friends, saying,
'This is my body given for you.
This is my blood shed for you.
Eat and drink to remember me.'

As we share your life in this bread and this cup,
may we, with all the faithful in this place,
be set aflame with your love,
and filled with your power,
that others may see
and be drawn to you,
and live to your glory and praise. **Amen.**

At a baptism

Jesus said, 'I am the way, the truth and the life.'

Before the name 'Christian' was used, in the early years of the Church's life, followers of Jesus were known as people of the Way.

As you grow up, and begin to discover what it means to live the Jesus Way, you might like to ponder these truths, which we who were present at your baptism pass on to you.

First, you are precious to God (Isaiah 43.4). Nothing you can do, no circumstances of your life can alter that. You may turn away from God, but God will never stop loving you, and will always welcome you back.

Then, you have a relationship with the created world. 'Consider the birds,' Jesus said (Matthew 6.26). Look at the flowers, marvel at the wonders of the created world, and the sustaining power of God which holds them in life. Let them remind you of your value. But being chosen and special does not mean being spoilt. We have a responsibility to the created world, and your relationship with God will challenge you to care for all that is around you, and use it with respect.

That leads to your relationship with people around you. They also are precious to God, and people who are on the Jesus Way are called to treat others as people who are loved, honoured and precious like us.

There will always be people on the Jesus Way to encourage you as you join in worship, read the Bible and learn to pray and reflect on your relationship with God and the world. But deeper than that is the love of God sustaining you, and the energy and life of God's Spirit filling you, and the friendship of Jesus as he walks with us all on the Way.

Have a good journey!

Eucharistic Prayer celebrating family life

Father of all,
we praise you that you have shown us
in the earthly life of your Son,
how love is nurtured and grown
in the testing ground of family life:
Help us to be faithful in our loving.

We praise you that in Jesus,
now risen and glorified,
you offer us fullness of life
beyond our imagining:
Raise us to life with him.

We praise you for the Spirit's
surprising presence, urging us on
to explore the riches of your love:
Open our hearts to your transforming power.

Open us up to your glory, Lord, as
with angels and archangels and
all who through the ages
have responded to your call,
we praise you, saying:
Holy, holy, holy Lord,
God of love and joy;
Heaven and earth are full of your glory,
all praise to your name.

Come now, Lord, and make your dwelling
in our hearts and homes,
as we remember Jesus, who
on the night before his death,
took bread and wine, blessed them
and gave them to his friends, saying,

'This is my body, given for you.
This is my blood, shed for you.
Eat and drink to remember me.'

Come freshly to us, living God,
and through these gifts of bread and wine
nourish us with your life.

In all the changes we experience
steady us with your faithfulness.

In all our relationships
inspire us with your love.

May our families and our homes
be signs of your kingdom:
Your kingdom come in us, Lord,
and transform the world
to your praise and glory. Amen.

Harvest

Celebrating harvest goes very deep in us – it seems to stir in us a sense of our country roots, memories of a land that lived by agriculture before the Industrial Revolution turned most of us into townies. Some of us don't have to go very far back to find our farming connections. My mother was a farmer's daughter, and she talked about the Harvest Home celebrations, when the big table that our branch of the family inherited was connected by a spare leaf to another like it, and all at the farm marked the end of the harvest with a party.

Although none of us has done it, probably, we sing 'We plough the fields and scatter the good seed on the land', and it doesn't seem in the least odd, even though farmers are much more efficient in their methods now. Harvest marks the end of a sequence in the church/country calendar. Plough Sunday in January, when the farm implements were blessed; Rogation Days just before Ascension Day in May, when prayers were made for favourable weather for the growing crops; Lammas Day at the beginning of August, when the first loaf made with flour from the new crop was offered in token thanks, and coming full circle, (though it was introduced much later on the liturgical scene, in the nineteenth century) Harvest. Time for a pause before it all starts again. Time to be thankful, to remember God's mercy and goodness, enjoying the sight of full storehouses and barns, pantry shelves and freezers. Time to feel secure against the coming winter. It is good to be thankful, and we come gladly, enjoying the colour, the smells and, with luck, a party.

But there's something uncomfortable about Harvest, too, especially now that we can see on our television screens that there are people who haven't got a harvest to celebrate, some who haven't had a harvest for years, perhaps because the rains have failed, perhaps because civil wars have made it impossible to cultivate the land. The Jewish people faced the same situation on a smaller scale. Reading the instructions in Deuteronomy we are reminded that God's people have always been told to be generous, and help the poor to share our good fortune. Deuteronomy speaks of very different farming methods, but the message is clear: don't keep it all to yourself, leave something for those in need.

And the New Testament warns us against taking things for granted, being pleased with our achievement. That man who pulled down his barn and built a bigger one, stuffed it full and sat back feeling pleased with himself got a sharp reminder – 'You fool! This very night your life is being demanded of you. And the things you have prepared, whose will they be?' (Luke 12.16–21). That's the question Harvest asks us too.

In the Bible, harvest and judgement go together – the parable of the wheat and the tares puts the point very starkly (Matthew 13.24–30). So it's right and good to be thankful, but we have to ask ourselves how our thankfulness can find expression in making it possible for all humankind to be thankful. We can't ever sit back and say we've done enough – not while there are all those children with stick limbs and swollen bellies looking at us hopelessly from our screens.

If we are going to be on the side of the angels, we have to work for the elimination of hunger, and the inhumanity which locks most of the world's food away from those who need it most. We have to support the agencies who work to improve farming methods, but we also need to put our political will behind the removal of world debt, an issue which keeps on being pushed down the agenda by scandals and atrocities across the world. We must keep asking the questions and seeking action. Harvest is the point where, far from sitting back and thinking how fortunate we are, we have to prepare to sow the seeds and encourage the growth for the harvest to come, when the will of God will be done on earth, as it is in heaven.

St Michael and All Angels

Would you recognize an angel if you saw one? I suppose we all think we would, because we've seen pictures of them so often. Painters and sculptors have given us the conventions: wings, floating robes, haloes. So we know how to portray even the most un-angelic if we want them to be angels: children look so different when dressed for the part. But we only have to see them out of costume, being children, to recognize that the stage props can be misleading.

Perhaps we come closer to recognizing an angel when we say, in response to an act of kindness, 'Oh, you are an angel!' Or to persuade someone to do an act of kindness we say, 'Be an angel.' But the Bible opens our eyes to angelic presence with a harder edge, and in more guises than we have always recognized.

Angels

Flames of fire, shafts of illumination;
Disconcerting messengers of God;
Assuring a woman that she can give birth;
Telling a man that what she bears is
Gift from God; challenging us to
Look, and not seek life where only death
Is found; opening doors, surrounding us with
Care, surprising us into fresh understanding.[1]

Since about 500 AD, the heavenly host has been divided into nine 'Orders', in three groups of three. In the top rank are the *Seraphim*, the six-winged creatures whose work is the praise of God, ceaselessly chanting, 'Holy, holy, holy' (Isaiah 6.3). They are accompanied by the *Cherubim*, guardians of the truth and the presence of God. Cherubim (the word is plural) were stationed at the gateway to Eden, to guard the way to the tree of life, and placed at each end of the Ark of the

Covenant to guard the place where God was thought to be specially present. They were strong creatures, with no resemblance to the *putti* beloved of baroque artists (Genesis 3.24; Exodus 25.18–22; 2 Samuel 22.10–13; Psalm 18.10; 80.1; 99.1). The third group in this first rank were called *Thrones*, the great wheels or many-eyed ones, sometimes acting as chariots. There's a description of their likeness in Ezekiel's vision of the appearance of God at the beginning of his book (Ezekiel 1). And when Elisha's servant got frightened in battle, Elisha prayed that his eyes would be opened, and he saw the chariots of fire surrounding the armies, outnumbering the enemy by far (2 Kings 6.17).

In the middle group of three are *Dominions*, (angels of mercy) *Virtues* (angels of blessing) and *Powers* (on the borders of heaven guarding against demonic intervention). These are only mentioned in passing in Scripture, but were part of ancient thinking.

In the last group are *Principalities*, originally protectors of nations and cities, and the *Archangels* and *Angels*, the two Orders which have direct dealings with humans.

Sanctus

Should you hear them singing among stars
or whispering secrets of a wiser world,
do not imagine ardent fledgling children.
They are intelligences old as sunrise
that never learnt left from right,
    before from after,
knowing but one direction, into God,
    but one duration, now.
Their melody strides not from bar to bar,
but like a painting hangs there entire
one chord of limitless communication.
You have heard it in the rhythms of the hills,
the spiralling turn of a dance, the
    fall of words

or the touch of fingers at the right,
  rare moment,
and these were holy, holy.

John V. Taylor[2]

We know the names of three Archangels from the Bible: Michael, remembered for his great battle against evil (Daniel 10.13, 12.1; Revelation 12.7–9); Gabriel who played such an active part in the events surrounding Jesus' birth (Luke 1 and 2); and Raphael concerned with healing (Tobit 3.17). Uriel is named in Jewish tradition. Other traditions name Metatron and Azael. There seem to have been seven Archangels, but the names of the remaining three vary in different traditions.

The Angels are those who have most dealings with humans. The word 'angel' means 'messenger', and the Angels are around in the biblical story surprising people into new understanding of God's ways with humanity. They are not always immediately recognized, and they bring challenge as well as comfort. They move with ease between earth and heaven, putting their worship into practice by ensuring that God's purposes are carried out on earth (Genesis 18.1–16; 28.10–17; Numbers 22 and 23; Matthew 13.37–42, 47–50; 18.10; Acts 10.1–8; 12.1–11; 27.21–25; Hebrews 13.2; Revelation 5.11–14).

It is in the company of all these heavenly beings that we live our lives, and they challenge us in our commitment. There is no doubt where their priority lies: it is in worship. But worship is only complete when the whole of existence is directed to putting God first. We are caught up in the continuing conflict between good and evil: events around us provide plenty of evidence that evil is alive and rotten in our world. But our faith is that the power of love and good is stronger, and we are invited to join the work of the Angels by putting that faith into practice. We are called to challenge oppression and injustice, and to work for peace. These sound like global politics, and so they are. But they are also the stuff of ordinary life, as we interact with our fellow humans.

The Angels are God's messengers, listening for God's word, and acting on it. We are invited to join them in their listening, and then help those around us to hear as well. The Angels are symbols of God's continuing care for his creation, care in which we are also involved.

Angels are part of the poetry of God's love. Poetry doesn't define or prescribe, but opens our eyes to new understanding. Lord, open our minds and our hearts, and keep us faithful in your love.

(Ideas from the preceding reflection can be developed into a workshop, using art, music and poetry, and providing opportunity for creative work, both in artistic areas and in looking at involvement in work for peace and justice.)

Notes

1. *Watching for the Kingfisher*, p. 31.
2. Previously unpublished. Used with permission.

Suffering

Suffering is probably the biggest challenge our faith will encounter. We are all puzzled by it, have difficulty in making sense of it, fear it, resent it, and wonder where, if at all, it fits into God's will.

None of us escapes suffering. We experience loss and pain, and we watch others suffer too, whether remotely, through the awful pictures on TV of starving, homeless people in Africa or in countries ravaged by war or natural disasters, or in our own families as illness or despair, or loss of independence in the diminishments of old age, bite deeper. We want to know *why*? We want to know how long it's going to go on. We hate the feeling that we're not in control.

Like many people, I've struggled with these questions, and wrestled with God in the pain of human experience. Perhaps, though, the most important thing is not what we end up saying about suffering, but what we end up saying about God.

There is a deep-seated strand of thinking that persists in saying that God sends suffering to test us. I find that hard to square with the God revealed in Jesus Christ, who made it quite plain that suffering is *not* what God wants. Jesus *healed* the sick, *challenged* the people who oppressed others. 'I came that [people] may have life,' he said (John 10.10).

Nor is it easy to square what we know of God in Jesus with another prevalent idea, that somehow we deserve what we get. We rebel almost instinctively against that thought – 'What have I done to deserve this?' we say. The answer is usually, 'nothing'. Of course, there is suffering we bring on ourselves – but it is a consequence of *our* actions, rather than a punishment from God. How can those starving children in Africa deserve such suffering? How have victims of murder come to deserve their fate? Some suffering is caused by sin, but it is not the sin of those who suffer, but the sin of those who hold life cheap.

So, if suffering is not a test, and not something we deserve, why does it happen, and why doesn't God do something to prevent it? This question was focused for me very sharply during the years when I was caring for my mother as she moved further and further into the confusion of senile dementia. She ceased to be the person we had known; she didn't know who she was, or who anyone else was, and the disintegration was awful to watch. Her freedom and wholeness, and ours, would only come through death – but she showed no signs of dying.

One day, while she was struggling with this existence, as I walked to work, a man dropped dead in front of me. I learnt during the day that he was a man in his fifties, who had left a widow, and two sons just about to start at university. Where was the sense in that death? There was my mother still going on in her twilight existence, and this man who had gone out to work that morning apparently with quite a lot of useful life ahead of him, suddenly dead. It seemed a cruel irony.

'You must be left with some questions,' said a friend when I told him what had happened. True, but in the end it was only one question. Did God know what he was doing? I've already said that I don't believe God sends suffering as a test or for any other reason. I desperately wanted God to intervene and put an end to my mother's suffering. But that raised another problem, because I don't believe in that sort of God either. God has given the universe laws which it has to follow, and there was no reason why they should be varied for me or for my mother. I did not doubt that God was in it all somewhere; the question was, where? (It is, of course, more complex than that, because God does sometimes apparently intervene!)

Gradually I came to a fresh understanding. I had been brought up with a vocabulary which only used words like almighty, powerful, omnipotent, in connection with God. I needed new words, like vulnerable, and suffering. An all-powerful God who makes people suffer, or who acts capriciously, would not be a God worth worshipping. But a God who has made himself vulnerable by offering us responsibility, and giving us free will; who suffers with us, and is brought to his knees with us, and who continually brings new life out of dead ends, that's a God I can relate to. Not obviously omnipotent, but skilled in crisis management. God's will is that people should be whole, and his will is constantly thwarted by illness, suffering, loss and death. And in all this, God suffers too, helping us to bear the pain and find signs of hope.

So when I in turn became ill, I felt that God and I had been here before, in a situation not of his will, and certainly not my choice, and that the way through was to hang on to God's faithfulness, in it with me, sharing the pain, holding me in love. Perhaps that's what taking up our cross means: being faithful to our commitment to the God we worship, finding God in the midst of whatever life throws at us.

'Christ in you, the hope of glory' (Colossians 1.27). We read those words sometimes in a triumphalist way, as though we've already got to the glory. But Paul was writing about hope, which always relates to something ahead of us. And he wrote it in the context of our suffering being part of Christ's suffering. It is the Christ who suffered and stayed faithful whom we meet in our pain. In his brokenness, in Gethsemane and the cross, he speaks to our vulnerability and calls us to himself. We can never say, 'God, you don't know what it's like to suffer.' In Jesus, God shows us that he does know.

Prayer for healing

'I came that they may have life, and have it abundantly.' (John 10.10)

We all long for that, but how do we achieve it? Some people put their trust in something like the Lottery – fullness of life, they say, will be possible when we can pay off all our debts and buy all we want. But those who pray for healing acknowledge that there are deeper needs than those for which money can provide. Good though it might be to be out of debt, able to do what we want without having to go without something else, deep down we know that we have other needs.

The ministry of prayer for healing and wholeness is a way of addressing those needs which the Church has encouraged right from the early days. James 5.13–16 indicates that this ministry was a part of Church practice from an early stage. It sprang out of a realization that healing lay at the heart of Jesus' ministry, as he healed physical and emotional pain, eased strained relationships with forgiveness, and encouraged people to realize that God's love is stronger than whatever may be disturbing us.

But what is healing? It is probably helpful to recognize that it is not necessarily the same as a cure. In some Christian traditions, you would expect to find a heap of crutches or hearing aids left behind after a service of prayer for healing, because they were no longer necessary. That may happen, but if it doesn't, it won't mean that healing hasn't taken place.

I learnt most about the difference between healing and cure when my father was diagnosed with cancer. At first I prayed very hard that he would get better. But his cancer was too far advanced for that, and however hard I prayed, it soon became obvious that he was going to die – and the longer he lived, the more he would suffer. Gradually my prayer changed, as I began to realize that for him, healing would only come through death. And perhaps that's always the truth, that only death will give us the freedom to be truly whole. It wasn't easy to accept. I often felt very angry. And part of my healing was to realize that it is all right to be angry with God. God is big enough to take it – that's part of what the cross is about.

God was at work then, changing my father, changing me, changing the family, leading us all on to something new. Although there was no cure (my father died), I'm sure there was healing. It showed in my father's courage in facing pain and death; it showed in the way we as a family were drawn closer together and began to be able to express our love for each other more openly; it showed in the way we were set free from fear and anxiety. That doesn't mean that his death didn't hurt – it was a painful letting go all round. But it led on to something new. Healing doesn't mean going back to what one was before, it's a growing on to a new stage. It can be painful and costly as the growth takes us through many deaths and resurrections on our way to life.

Healing may take us by surprise – after one healing service I attended, a woman who was going blind said, 'I know I'm going blind, but after tonight, I'm not so afraid.' Prayer for healing means opening ourselves up to God's love, asking God to give us what God knows we need, rather than putting a lot of energy into asking for what we want. We might do well to remember those four men who brought their paralysed friend to Jesus, with energy that let nothing stand in their way (Mark 2.1–12). No doubt they wanted their friend to walk again but, wisely, they didn't restrict Jesus' actions by saying so. They let Jesus deal with what lay at the root of the man's illness, and Jesus set him free from whatever it was that had left him helpless, literally without a leg to stand on, for so long.

So, we come asking for healing, perhaps knowing our need, perhaps with a sense of need we can't put into words. Or we might come because, like those four men, we want to bring someone else to Jesus for his healing touch. We might come in gratitude that we are being healed, with a longing that our spiritual life will be strengthened and deepened.

The result of our prayer will be an expression of God's love for us. It may be the disappearance of whatever is troubling us, it may be a new appreciation of our own worth; it may be a new determination to work for social changes that will bring wholeness to others; it may be fresh courage to face an old situation. We may not be aware that anything has happened until later. But God will respond with his healing gifts at whatever level we can receive them. And then we go out to offer his healing to those around us, for healing is not just for individuals. I can't be whole while my brothers and sisters in the world are in need. Part of the healing we must pray for is that society, ours and others', and our church communities too, will change so that all people will be free to find their wholeness. Part of our wholeness will come as we work for the peace, freedom and justice which are God's will for us all.

Give thanks – always?

Thank you. That's one of the first things children learn to say. And it's fine when we can see what it is we have to be thankful for. One of the things I remember from my childhood was writing thank-you letters. Christmas and birthdays brought lots of gifts, but the downside was writing the letters in response. I don't know whether children still go through the same discipline – it's so easy to pick up the phone, or let mum or dad do it for you.

I was quite happy to write when the gift was something I appreciated, but it wasn't so easy when the donor didn't seem to have remembered who I was. One of my aunts always caused difficulties. She sent me a doll's hot-water bottle once, apparently unaware that I was 12 years old that birthday!

Saying thank you can be problematic – you probably know the series of letters by John Julius Norwich, purporting to have been written by Emily to Edward in response to the gifts sent on the 12 days of Christmas, ending with a broken engagement, and a solicitor's letter restraining Edward from sending further gifts.

Against that background of experience, we find ourselves reminded to give thanks to God the Father at all times and for everything in the name of our Lord Jesus Christ (Ephesians 5.20). When we count our blessings, we find that there are far more than we thought. But that isn't the whole of our experience. How do we thank God when we are in the middle of one of those awful patches when it doesn't look as though there is much to be thankful for: when life falls apart at the death of a loved one, or the loss of a job; when health deserts us, or hospital tests hang over us; when life loses its meaning, or the world situation seems so dire that we can't see much hope for the future?

What we can always give thanks for is God's faithfulness, holding us through all the darknesses and difficulties. We are not told to perform extraordinary emotional or mental gymnastics to persuade ourselves that somehow everything that happens is for the best. Jesus never gave the impression that somehow suffering would be good for us: he healed the sick, opposed all that destroyed people's lives, whether inner forces or those of society.

Jesus also made it clear that sometimes the only way to deal with suffering is to go through it and find, as he did at the end, that God has been holding us all the time. God's faithfulness to his people led him to enter into their suffering and pain, throughout their history but supremely in his engagement with the world in Jesus. We can never say, 'It's all right for you, God, you don't know what it's like.' God does know, he's in our circumstances, whatever they are, holding us in his profound love. And that is what we give thanks for, at all times and in all places.

One of the heroes of the Church is Polycarp, a bishop in Asia in the second century. He was martyred during one of the fiercest persecutions the Church experienced. When it became clear that the Roman officials were after him, he wanted to stay in the city and face them. His friends persuaded him to leave, and he went to a farm not far from the city, and spent his time in prayer, not for himself but, as his custom was, for the people of the world, and the churches in their mission to them. His respite was short-lived, and his pursuers caught up with him quite late on a Friday evening. Polycarp ordered that they should be given food and drink, and asked that they should give him an hour for prayer. In fact he prayed for two hours, and those who witnessed his prayer began to feel ashamed that they had come after so venerable an old man.

He was taken back to the city and, throughout the journey, his captors tried to persuade him to say, 'Caesar is Lord', and save himself. But he refused even to think of it. He was brought to the stadium and asked formally to swear allegiance to Caesar and curse Christ. Polycarp's response was to say, 'Eighty-six years I have served him, and he has done me no wrong. How then can I blaspheme my king who saved me?' So he was martyred.

'Eighty-six years I have served him, and he has done me no wrong.' We can all say that, whatever our age. God has done me no wrong. At all times and in all places, God's love never fails. That's the fact to hang on to, the reason for ever-growing thankfulness.

Remember, Remember, the theme of November

We remember many people in November: All Saints, All Souls, Guy Fawkes and, on Remembrance Day, all who have given their lives in war.

The festival of All Saints reminds us that we are part of a great company of people who have been touched by God, and have responded by living lives that in some measure give God glory. Saints are not extraordinarily holy people, so heavenly minded that they are no earthly use: weak, rather silly looking, with stained-glass haloes like dinner plates. All of us who have given our lives to God, however tentatively, are called saints in the New Testament. Look at the beginnings of Paul's letters, and think about what we know of the recipients. Take the Corinthians, for example, a more quarrelsome lot of people it would be hard to find. They argued amongst themselves and with Paul; they competed with each other about which were the best gifts to have, and which was the best leader to follow; they held services which were hardly a model of decorum; and they found it very difficult to work out how to apply their new faith to public life. Saints just like us, in fact.

Then comes the remembrance of All Souls, with the reminder that we are not only concerned with time and space, but with life beyond. Death is not 'nothing at all' as a popular reading at funerals suggests. Death is a very significant part of our life, which separates us, like birth at our beginning, from whatever lies beyond our conscious experience. All Souls Day is when we remember all those who have lived their lives and moved *on*, not *away*, but out of the spotlight.

We often think of time in a linear way. Bede records the conversation between Edwin, King of Northumbria in the seventh century, and his advisers when he was considering whether to adopt the Christian faith. One of the advisers, gesturing to the feasting hall in which they were assembled, with a central fire burning and unglazed windows gaping on to the darkness outside, suggested that human life is like that of a sparrow which flies into the feasting hall. For a short time it is in the light, but we don't know where it has come from or where it goes when it leaves. If this new faith tells us anything about the unseen world around us, then it is worth exploring (Bede, *Ecclesiastical History*, ch. XIII).

If we change the imagery from a line to a series of concentric circles, then our life is more like being on stage at a performance in the round, with all the people who have played their part, and those in the wings waiting to come on, watching with interest and some sympathy as we try to make sense of the script we have been given. And at the end, when the lights come up, we find the author of life's play is there to commend us, or perhaps to make a few suggestions about how our performance could have been improved. All Souls' Day reminds us of the unseen audience, some of whom we know and love for the way they have influenced our lives, for whom we give thanks along with all the others whom we don't know, but who share with us in God's love.

So we can be encouraged as we think of this great cloud of witnesses surrounding us on our journey, and renew our commitment to persevere in the race that lies ahead, looking to Jesus as we go (Hebrews 12.1–2).

Death – terminus or junction?

Ad Quem

Death – terminus,
Heart-stopping jolt
At the end of the line?
Or junction, where worlds meet,
Faith catching the connection?[1]

The one certain thing about us is that we will die. But we don't talk about death unless we have to. In our society we are cushioned from its reality. In spite of the number of violent deaths we see on our TV screens, many people have never seen or touched a dead person; and we keep being assured that steps are being taken to cut down the number of deaths from particular diseases, as though that will mean that some of us won't die at all.

It is good to work at eliminating pain and suffering, and it is natural to feel outrage at premature or violent death. But we seem to have great difficulty in accepting that death is a natural part of life. We have moved a long way from awareness of the natural rhythms of nature. Every year, the seasons remind us of new life growing to maturity and then moving towards death. Observation of the life of trees and plants teaches us that in order for life to continue, it has to progress from one stage to the next. A flower has to die before seed can be set. The seeds have to fall from the plant, apparently dead, before the next cycle of life can begin.

When I was a small child, I used to be puzzled when we prayed in church for people who were dangerously ill. In danger of what, I wondered. Presumably they were in danger of dying. But I also heard in church that there was something called eternal life, which seemed to be on the other side of death. Many years and experiences have intervened, and I've realized that things aren't that simple. Apart from the suffering that sometimes precedes death, there is always pain at the loss of people we love, and there are questions about what happens to us when we die.

Canon Henry Scott Holland, in a sermon preached at the Lying-in-State of Edward VII, said that we hover between two ways of regarding death. One is that death is the end. We recoil from this death, and protest at it, for it is unbearable to think that we shall never be able to talk to our loved ones, or touch them, again. Death is an insuperable barrier. The other view is that death is nothing at all. The person we loved is no longer there in the coffin in front of us, but they still exist. We go on thinking about them, praying for them, remembering them. This passage from the sermon is often read at funerals. It begins with the words 'Death is nothing at all.' But taken out of context, the passage is a denial of the reality we are experiencing when we are bereaved. Scott Holland went on to say that we may try to deny the fact of death, because it is so painful. But the sense of unreality we sometimes feel as we look at a dead body and realize that the person we loved is no longer there, will give way to the realization that far from being nothing at all, death is a hard reality which has made a difference. Our task, he said, is to reconcile both views of death: it is an end, but there is a continuity of growth in the love of God which enables this end to be a new beginning. The sermon was preached at Pentecost, and the preacher reminded his hearers that the gift of the Spirit was the gift of God's life experienced now, so that eternal life is not only life beyond the grave, but a life we begin to live here and now.

When we begin to grasp that idea, we have a new insight to offer. Death is not the worst thing that can happen to us. It is, rather, a natural stage in our growth. In the imagery of the poem at the beginning of this reflection, it is not a terminus but a junction, where worlds meet.

It is faith that catches the connection – and faith is not the same as certainty. Faith is an attitude of trust in the God who is always faithful. We learn that trust through many experiences of letting go in order that new life may grow. There are many deaths and resurrections on the way to fullness of life.

We don't know when we shall die – but we can prepare for it. 'From *sudden* death, Good Lord, deliver us' is a prayer (from the Book of Common Prayer), that we will be spared an *unprepared* death. There are, of course, practical things we can do to prepare for death, like making a will, and keeping our affairs in order so that our executors don't have too hard a task. But the deeper preparation lies in attending to our relationship with God, practising God's presence in our lives, making full use of the gift of life which is ours now, and which will grow into its fullness in God's love.

Year's mind

Every year, I pass the day
Not knowing. Someday
Someone will say, 'Oh yes,
Ann died a year ago.'

I pray they will remember
A day when I lived to the full,
A day of celebration
Of the gift of life.[2]

Notes

1. *Watching for the Kingfisher*, p. 111.
2. Ibid., p. 120.

Remembrance Day

Remembrance Day calls us to memories of the dead of two world wars, and the 60 or so years since of anything but peace. The numbers are mind-blowing, as we think of Africa, Europe, Ireland, the Middle East, in our lifetime. It has been said that if all who died in the First World War marched four abreast, when the head of the column reached the Cenotaph, the end would be at Durham; at the end of the Second War at Edinburgh. Who knows where it would be now, if we add all those who have died in battle since? And we remember not just the dead, but all who have suffered the living death of mental torture or physical disability.

Each year, as the time for remembrance comes round, very mixed emotions surface. For some, the pain and suffering they experience is still so great that all commemoration is tinged with bitterness. Talk of reconciliation and forgiveness provokes anger, and a feeling that no one understands the horror and brutality they witnessed or experienced. For others, the commemoration is the opportunity to acknowledge the horror of war, and pay tribute to those who sacrificed themselves, or were sacrificed, and to express gratitude for the measure of cooperation that has been achieved between nations who were formerly at each other's throats.

Others find themselves close to despair, because people seem to have learned so little. We've seen history repeating itself in the Balkans; we've seen a peace process that was conceived in such hope in Northern Ireland almost destroyed by people who can't let go of ancient feuds; we've seen unspeakable cruelty in parts of Africa; and then there's Afghanistan, and Iraq, and the Middle East. The list could go on. And it won't include only things that happen outside the UK. What has happened to the vision of 'a world fit for heroes to live in' we ask, as we look at the homeless, the helpless, the despised in our own society.

What is the point of remembering if we don't learn from

what we remember? It has been said that history repeats itself because we don't learn the lessons the first time round. Remembering has to be coupled with action for a better world. One of the tasks the gospel calls us to is that of peace-making. That can sound very bland, pouring oil on troubled waters, pretending that as long as everything looks all right on the surface, all is well.

To be a peacemaker is to be at the cutting edge of relationships, where, as we draw closer together in our common humanity, we take forgiveness seriously. One of the first things to recognize about forgiveness is that we all need it. None of us belongs to a race with absolutely clean hands. All participants in war do terrible things to each other. We have to stop looking for someone else to blame, and look at where our responsibility lies. We have to recognize that within each of us there is the potential for evil as well as for good – and if we haven't behaved all that badly as individuals, let's give thanks that the grace of God has been at work in us.

What, then, is forgiveness? We sometimes talk about it as though it is easy. 'Forgive and forget,' we say. 'Let bygones be bygones.' But we can't forget something that has devastated us, either in war or in personal circumstances. Forgiveness does not mean letting people off as though what they have done doesn't matter, and it doesn't exclude due punishment. Forgiveness means setting people free. Forgiveness is not forgetting, it's learning to remember differently. It's saying, 'What happened was evil, and it hurt, but I'm not going to let it poison my life any more.' When we can say that, we set ourselves free, too. Forgiveness starts with us being changed. It's not easy or cheap, but it's the way to the life of fullness and peace, the life to which God invites us.

There are many examples of people who have learned the truth of that in their own experience. Eric Lomax is one, and he tells his story in the book *The Railway Man.*[1] He suffered imprisonment and torture while the Burma/Siam Railway was being built, and was left at the end of the war with a terrible anger against those who had tortured him, especially the man who had acted as the interpreter at his interrogations. His story tells how, eventually, Eric came face to face with that man who, like himself, was scarred and haunted by his experience. Eric commented that he realized that there came a point where the hating had to stop.

Being a peacemaker means taking life seriously, facing up to its pain, and helping people set each other free from memories that lock them into hatred. And that's not easy. When Jesus tried living in a spirit of forgiveness, he was crucified, and he carries the scars for eternity. But it's better to have scars than running sores.

So we remember. We remember those killed in war, and those scarred by war, with deep gratitude for the sacrifices they and their families made. The red poppy will always be a symbol of that. And we remember so that we take the lessons of history to heart. A white poppy is worn by a growing number of people as a sign of commitment to justice and peace. Red and white poppies are not alternatives, but complement each other.

And we remember because it's one of the great Bible words, calling us back again and again to God's faithfulness, and his will that his people should live in love. And each time we meet for a Eucharist, we remember Jesus who suffered and was raised to life so that we might have life in all its fullness. Let's open ourselves up to the possibility that life really can be different because we remember.

Note

1. Eric Lomax, *The Railway Man*, Vintage Books, 1996.

For thine is the kingdom

The Church's year ends with the festival of Christ the King.

The kingdom of God is what the whole year has been about. But what comes to mind when we hear the words 'king' or 'kingdom'? Perhaps other words like power, wealth, glamour, lands, possessions, banquets – mostly words that are remote from our experience. The British Royal Family has made valiant efforts to be less remote, but we still find it hard to think of the Royals as people like us: it is difficult to think of the Queen queuing at a supermarket checkout, Prince Philip running for a bus, or the royal children eating fish and chips out of newspaper.

We are asked to celebrate Christ as King, just at the point when the Christian Church is moving towards the celebration of Christmas, when God came to live in the world as one of us. We won't be able to do it if we think about Jesus as a king in the tradition of our historical monarchs. Jesus told us that we need to turn our ideas about kingship upside down, if we are really going to understand how he is King.

The way had been prepared for the new style of kingship by the prophets. Jeremiah, for example, had said (Jeremiah 23.1–6) that the rulers had not looked after their people properly, and so a new king was coming, sent by God, who would really care for his people. And then Jesus came and said to anyone who would listen, 'The time is fulfilled, and the kingdom of God has come near; repent and believe in the good news' (Mark 1.15). The good news was, is, that God is creating something new, turning our ideas round, turning us round. For that is what repentance means, quite simply 'turning round'.

Jesus talked a great deal about the kingdom, and he made it quite clear that God's kingdom is not like the kingdoms that his hearers knew about, where the ruler was all powerful, and the people knuckled under or took the consequences. The king/lord/master in Jesus' stories was not a despot, ordering people around for his own pleasure, but someone who respected what people had to offer and repeatedly gave them opportunities to grow and flourish. All were welcome in his kingdom, except those who oppressed and ill-treated others. For example, the man in one of Jesus' stories who was let off an enormous debt, and then tried to throttle someone who owed him very little got short shrift (Matthew 18.23–35). So did the person who was so jealous of other people's gifts that he refused to use his own, and buried it to keep it safe until he could hand it back to his master undeveloped (Matthew 25.14–30).

God's kingdom is the realization, the making real, of a vision of life where everyone achieves their potential. Jesus worked to establish that kingdom. He challenged people into new ways of thinking; he removed some of the obstacles to people's growth to fullness of life, sometimes by healing physical or mental illness, sometimes by healing spiritual disease by offering acceptance of people as they were, encouraging them to believe that God's love could embrace even them. The dying thief we read about in Luke 23.39–43 was only the last in a long line of people like Zacchaeus, and Peter, lepers and others on the edge of society. Wherever people responded, the kingdom of God began to arrive. The kingdom is very near – but it is not here yet.

There's a lovely little cameo in Mark's Gospel (Mark 12.41–44), where Jesus pointed to a widow who was giving all that she had – not calculating how much of her life she would offer, not even telling others what she was doing, just getting on with offering her life to God. If we all did that, the world would be a very different place. And, of course, we have begun to make that offering – though we know in our hearts that the kingdom of complete response to God is some way off. But the kingdom is coming: it begins to be a reality wherever people adopt the kingdom values of love and justice, forgiveness and living in peace.

When we pray, 'Your kingdom come', it is not only a prayer about what needs to happen in the lives of other people.

It is a prayer about what needs to happen in us. That's where it has to start. 'Repent,' said Jesus. Keep turning round to focus on God. That's what Advent will call us to again. May your kingdom come in us, Lord. Transform us, and through us all whom we meet and influence, to your glory.

Copyright Acknowledgements

The author and publisher gratefully acknowledge the use of copyright items. Every effort has been made to trace copyright owners, but where we have been unsuccessful we would welcome information which would enable us to make appropriate acknowledgement in any reprint.

Section 1

pp. 21–2 Psalm by Robin Harger, written in a workshop at a parish weekend. Used with permission.

p. 50 Michael Lloyd, *Café Theology*, Alpha International, 2005.

p. 50 Robert Frost, 'Mending Wall', *North of Boston*, Henry Holt and Co, 1915.

p. 50 Edwin Markham, 'Outwitted' *The Shoes of Happiness and Other Poems*, University of Michigan Press, 1915.

Section 2

p. 101 W. H. Frere prayer, used with permission of the Community of the Resurrection, Mirfield.

pp. 115–16 John V. Taylor, *A Matter of Life and Death*, SCM Press, 1986, p. 49, used with permission of the Estate of John V. Taylor.

Section 3

pp. 238–9 John V. Taylor, 'Sanctus' (Christmas card poem 1993), unpublished. Used with permission of the Estate of John V. Taylor.